BARBARA RUIZ

RICE

DISHES OF THE WORLD

BARBARA RUIZ

RICE

DISHES
OF
THE
WORLD

ABSOLUTE PRESS

First published in 1990 by Absolute Press, 14 Widcombe Crescent, Bath BA2
6AH, England.

Design: Ian Middleton

Illustrations: Caroline Nisbett

ISBN 0 948230 25 8

Printed by Longdunn Press Ltd, Bristol

CONTENTS

TYPES OF RICE

PATNA – A good long grain all purpose rice which was originally grown in India but is now imported mostly from the USA.

ARBORIO – A short, round grain from Northern Italy, perfect for risottos.

BASMATI – A long, delicate grain with a distinctive taste, from India and Pakistan, ideal for serving with curries and other Indian dishes.

BROWN RICE – The natural, whole grain from which only the outer husk has been removed. It is high in fibre and retains its flavour and 'bite' after cooking.

NOTE

Measurements for rice throughout the book are given in fluid ounces to make it compatible with the measurement of the liquid in which the rice is to be cooked.

INTRODUCTION

In Java a girl is only regarded as ready to marry when she knows how to cook a bowl of rice. Rice as a symbol of fecundity and plenty is eaten at festivals in the East to bring long life, happiness and abundance (and of course thrown at the bride and bridegroom in Western countries).

Nowadays much refining and polishing and creating of new rice products is going on with the strictly commercial aim of tempting the palate. Fortunately campaigns for healthy eating have favoured the consumption of the whole grain, so giving us back the whole goodness of this food.

I have collected these recipes not only by gathering together my home rice recipes, but also by travelling abroad.

I was brought up in a home where rice was a regular dish to accompany meat or pulses. I loved it, but I never imagined the immense variety of rice dishes I was to discover later; my travels in Europe and Asia have been a revelation. I went about on my holidays tasting wonderful new rice dishes and writing down recipes from friends, restaurants, friends of friends and cooks. On one occasion someone sent me a recipe on a postcard of the town where we had eaten a delicious rice. Sometimes I was invited to dinner when an exciting new rice dish was served. On these occasions I was always determined to get the recipe for my collection. Once back home I would cook the newly learned rice dishes, remembering flavours and trying recipes until I got the right taste. So I went from the exuberant Spanish paella and the delicate and delicious Italian risottos to the exotic Indian and Hunzakut rice dishes.

My experience grew as I travelled and the recipes piled up with the years. I have shared my rice dishes with my family and friends. Now I want to share these recipes with you in the hope that you will cook and enjoy them as well.

STARTERS

PEPPERS STUFFED WITH RICE

INGREDIENTS

3½ OZ (100G) BROWN RICE

4 TABLESPOONS OLIVE OIL

1 MEDIUM ONION, CHOPPED

1 CLOVE GARLIC, CRUSHED

9 OZ (250G) MINCED LAMB

1 OZ (25G) HAM, FINELY CHOPPED

2 TOMATOES, PEELED AND CHOPPED

½ TEASPOON DRIED OREGANO

1 TABLESPOON PINE NUTS

1 TABLESPOON CHOPPED PARSLEY

SALT AND PEPPER

4 LARGE GREEN OR RED PEPPERS

3 TABLESPOONS BEEF STOCK OR COLD WATER

YOU CAN HAVE PEPPERS STUFFED WITH RICE AS A STARTER OR AS A LIGHT LUNCH ACCOMPANIED BY A GREEN SALAD.

SERVES 4

First cook the rice in plenty of slightly salted boiling water until it is just tender. Drain and put aside. Heat the oil and sauté the onion and garlic. Add the lamb and ham and stir around for 2 minutes. Then add the tomatoes, oregano and pine nuts and cook for a few more minutes. Add the parsley and the rice with salt and pepper to taste. Remove from the heat and set aside.

Wash the peppers, cut off the tops and remove the seeds. Fill the peppers with the rice mixture and place them, closely packed, in a baking dish. Spoon 3 tablespoons of beef stock if you have it, or cold water, into the dish. Bake the stuffed peppers in a pre-heated oven at 375F/190C/Gas 5 for 30–40 minutes. You can serve this dish with tomato sauce if you wish.

TOMATOES STUFFED WITH RICE

SERVES 2

First cook the rice in plenty of slightly salted boiling water. Cook until it is just tender and drain. Rinse under running cold water and drain again.

Flake the anchovies and add to the rice. Stir in the garlic and herbs and add salt and pepper to taste. Wash the tomatoes, slice off the round ends and scoop out the core and seeds. Put a little olive oil and pepper into the hollow tomatoes and fill them with the rice mixture. Place the stuffed tomatoes in a roasting tin. Spoon 3 tablespoons of water into the tin and sprinkle a teaspoon of olive oil on top of the tomatoes. Bake them in a pre-heated oven at 350F/180C/Gas 4 for 25 minutes.

3½ OZ (100G) LONG GRAIN WHITE RICE

1 TIN ANCHOVIES

1 CLOVE GARLIC, CRUSHED

¼ TEASPOON DRIED OREGANO

½ TABLESPOON CHOPPED PARSLEY

½ TABLESPOON CHOPPED BASIL

¼ TEASPOON MARJORAM

SALT AND PEPPER

4 LARGE FIRM BEEF TOMATOES

OLIVE OIL

AUBERGINES STUFFED WITH RICE

2 OZ (50G) BROWN RICE

2 LARGE AUBERGINES

2 FL OZ (50ML) OLIVE OIL

2 CLOVES GARLIC, CRUSHED

2 MEDIUM ONIONS, FINELY CHOPPED

½ TEASPOON GROUND CUMIN

½ TEASPOON GROUND CINNAMON

2 TOMATOES, PEELED AND CHOPPED

½ OZ (10G) SULTANAS

½ OZ (10G) PINE NUTS

1 TABLESPOON CHOPPED PARSLEY, PLUS EXTRA TO GARNISH

SALT AND PEPPER

JUICE OF HALF A LEMON

1 TEASPOON CASTER SUGAR

THESE AUBERGINES STUFFED WITH RICE HAVE A DELICIOUS ORIENTAL TOUCH.

SERVES 4

Cook the rice in plenty of slightly salted boiling water until just tender. Drain and set aside. Clean the aubergines, chop off the tops and cut each in half lengthways. Spoon out the flesh without breaking the skin. Chop the flesh finely, sprinkle it with salt and place it in a colander. Weigh it down with a heavy dish and allow to stand for 45 minutes. Sprinkle the aubergine shells with salt and set aside.

Heat the oven to 350F/180C/Gas 4. Rinse the aubergine shells and flesh, drain well and pat dry with kitchen paper.

Heat the olive oil and fry the garlic, onion, cumin and aubergine flesh for about 5 minutes. Stir in the cinnamon and tomatoes and cook for 10 minutes or until the tomatoes have become a thick sauce. Remove from the heat and add the sultanas, pine nuts, parsley and salt and pepper. Stir in the rice and mix well.

Fill the aubergines with this mixture and place them, closely packed, in a baking tin. Pour hot water into the tin to come half way up to the sides of the stuffed aubergines. Add the lemon juice, sugar and some parsley stalks to the water.

Cover the tin with foil and bake for about 50–60 minutes. You can serve this dish cold or hot garnished with parsley.

RICE WITH MARINATED MUSHROOMS

AN EXCELLENT FIRST COURSE.

4 GIANT FLAT
MUSHROOMS

2 FL OZ (50ML) DRY
WHITE WINE

OLIVE OIL

SALT AND PEPPER

1 BAY LEAF

1 CLOVE GARLIC,
CRUSHED

1 SMALL ONION,
CHOPPED

4 FL OZ (125ML) WHITE
RICE

3 TABLESPOONS
MAYONNAISE

½ TABLESPOON FINELY
CHOPPED PARSLEY

SERVES 2

Clean the mushrooms, trim the stems and dry well. Place them in a glass bowl and cover with the wine. Let it stand for 2 hours. Lift the mushrooms out and cover them with olive oil mixed with salt and pepper in another glass bowl. Add the bay leaf, garlic and onion. Cover the bowl and let the mushrooms stand for 2 days.

After that, cook the rice in plenty of salted water. When tender, drain it well and let it cool. Add the mayonnaise to the rice. Lift the mushrooms from the oil mixture and fill them with the rice. Serve garnished with parsley.

SOUPS

VENEZUELAN RICE SOUP

INGREDIENTS

COOKING OIL

1 ONION, CHOPPED

2 CLOVES GARLIC, CRUSHED

3 TOMATOES, PEELED AND CHOPPED

3 PINTS (1.75 LITRES) BEEF STOCK

3 MEDIUM CARROTS, PEELED AND DICED

3½ OZ (100G) WHITE RICE

1 LARGE POTATO, PEELED AND DICED

SALT

1 TABLESPOON CHOPPED PARSLEY

In Venezuela it is customary to have soup as a first course. One of the old and traditional soups is rice soup. It is believed to have originated in the nineteenth century when it was popular in wayside inns where for a few pence people got generous bowls of this soup. I used to have Rice Soup at lunch time at my grandmother's home. This is a recipe that has been in my family for generations.

SERVES 4

Heat the oil in a saucepan and fry the onion and garlic for 2 minutes. Add the tomatoes and stir. Cook for a further 2 minutes. Add the stock and bring to the boil. Add the carrots and rice and cook gently for 10 minutes. Now add the diced potato and salt and cook until the rice and vegetables are tender. Add parsley, taste and add more seasoning if necessary. Serve hot.

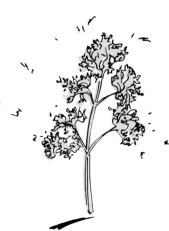

THICK RICE SOUP WITH LENTILS

A SOUP THAT IS FILLING ENOUGH TO SERVE AS A MAIN COURSE.

SERVES 4

First cook the green lentils in plenty of boiling water for 10 minutes. Drain and set aside.

Heat the oil in a saucepan and fry the onion and garlic for 1 minute. Add the cumin and bacon and stir around for another 2 minutes. Add the rice and lentils and stir carefully so that they are nicely coated. Then add the stock and salt and pepper to taste. Bring to the boil then lower the heat and cook gently until the rice and lentils are tender and the soup is thick. Now add the coriander leaves and allow to stand for 5 minutes before serving.

INGREDIENTS

3½ OZ (100G) GREEN LENTILS

OIL FOR FRYING

1 MEDIUM ONION, CHOPPED

2 CLOVES GARLIC, CRUSHED

½ TEASPOON GROUND CUMIN

2 RASHERS SMOKED BACON, FINELY CHOPPED

5 OZ (150G) WHITE RICE

2½ PINTS (1.4 LITRES) BEEF STOCK

SALT AND PEPPER

½ TEASPOON CHOPPED CORIANDER LEAVES

CHINESE SIZZLING RICE SOUP

INGREDIENTS

5 FL OZ (150ML) SHORT GRAIN RICE

10 FL OZ (275ML) BOILING WATER

SALT

1 PINT (570ML) FISH STOCK

8 OZ (225G) SHELLED PRAWNS

4 OZ (125G) MUSHROOMS, HALVED

2 TABLESPOONS DRY SHERRY

PINCH SUGAR

PINCH BLACK PEPPER

1 TABLESPOON SOY SAUCE

COOKING OIL

A Rice Soup that comes from Szechuan, in the West of China. Traditionally there are seven flavours associated with Szechuan cookery: Hot or la (chilli peppers), Fragrant or Xiang (ginger, garlic), Nutty or ma (sesame seeds), Sour or suan (vinegar), Bitter or ku (spring onion, scallion, leek), Salty or xien (soy sauce, salt), Sweet or tien (sugar, honey). The mixture of tien, xien and la gives this soup its special flavour. In Szechuan the cooked rice (paddies) for this dish is put out to dry in the sun, but since we cannot always count on the sun, the oven is a good substitute.

SERVES 4

Pour the boiling water on to the rice. Add salt, put a lid on and bring to the boil. Lower the heat, cook gently for about 15 minutes then set aside.

Bring the stock to boil in a pan and add the prawns, mushrooms, salt, sherry, sugar, pepper and soy sauce. Cover with a lid, lower the heat and simmer for approximately 10 minutes. Set aside and keep hot.

Now spread the cooked rice in an even layer on a greased baking sheet, press down and put to dry in a slow oven until brittle. Cut the rice into pieces of about 3 inches (7.5cm). Next heat the oil and fry the pieces of rice until crispy. To serve, put 2 or 3 pieces of rice in individual bowls and pour the soup over the rice. The sizzling that follows makes this rice dish a conversation piece.

RICE AND COURGETTE SOUP

THIS SOUP HAS A VERY DELICATE FLAVOUR AND IS
WONDERFULLY EASY TO PREPARE.

SERVES 4

Start by heating the oil in a saucepan. Fry the onion, garlic and
celery for a minute or two. Add the carrot and courgettes
and stir around. Let it cook for a minute, then add the
tomatoes and cook for a further 4 minutes. Now add the rice
and the chicken stock. Add salt to taste, bring to the boil,
lower the heat and cook gently until the rice and vegetables
are tender. Sprinkle the parsley over the soup and serve at
once.

COOKING OIL

1 MEDIUM ONION,
CHOPPED

1 CLOVE GARLIC,
CRUSHED

1 STICK CELERY,
CHOPPED

1 MEDIUM CARROT,
DICED

5 COURGETTES,
CLEANED AND DICED

3 TOMATOES, PEELED
AND CHOPPED

3½ OZ (100G) WHITE
RICE

3 PINTS (1.75 LITRES)
CHICKEN STOCK

SALT

1 TABLESPOON
CHOPPED PARSLEY

OLLETA (South American Rice Soup)

INGREDIENTS

1 OX HEART

1 OX LIVER, SOAKED IN
MILK FOR 2 HOURS

1 OX TAIL, JOINTED

2½ PINTS (1.4 LITRES)
WATER

COOKING OIL

1 MEDIUM ONION,
CHOPPED

2 CLOVES GARLIC,
CRUSHED

5 CLOVES

2 LARGE TOMATOES,
PEELED AND CHOPPED

1 LEVEL TEASPOON
MUSCOVADO SUGAR

4 FL OZ (125ML) RED
WINE

2 OZ (50G) WHITE RICE

The word OLLETA comes from the Spanish OLLA which means pot or hotpot. Olleta used to be a Sunday soup in poor homes when people could buy offal at butcher's shops for very little. Sometimes instead of offal they made do with a cock as the flavour of the cock was the best substitute for offal. Few people in Venezuela nowadays know how to prepare Olleta which is a pity since this soup is not only delicious and substantial, but has a very special flavour all of its own.

SERVES 5−6

Cut the heart and the liver into small pieces and place them with the ox tail in a pan. Add the water, cover and bring to the boil. Lower the heat and cook on a medium heat for about 1−1½ hours. Add a little more water if necessary.

Then in a saucepan heat 3 tablespoons of oil and fry the onion and the garlic. Stir for 1 minute and add the cloves and tomatoes. Stir for a few more minutes. Now add the sugar and the wine. Stir the mixture then pour into the soup. Add the rice and adjust seasoning. Cook for a further 20−25 minutes.

Serve the Olleta on earthenware dishes with some crusty bread.

MAIN DISHES

PLAIN BOILED RICE

16 FL OZ (425ML) WATER

SALT

8 FL OZ (225ML) LONG
GRAIN WHITE RICE

SERVES 4

Bring the water with a pinch of salt to the boil and add the
rice. Cover with a lid and as soon as it starts boiling again,
lower the heat and let the rice cook very gently for 15
minutes or until it is tender and dry. Do not take the lid off
or stir the rice while it is cooking. Serve with a knob of
butter if you wish.

GARLIC AND ONION RICE

INGREDIENTS

1 OZ (25G) BUTTER

1 SMALL ONION,
CHOPPED

2 CLOVES GARLIC,
CRUSHED

10 FL OZ (275ML) BROWN
RICE

1 PINT (570ML) BOILING
WATER

SALT

SERVES 5

Melt the butter in a thick saucepan and soften the onion and
garlic, stirring with a wooden spoon. Next add the rice, stir it
around and pour on boiling water. Add salt, stir once more,
put on a lid and when it starts to boil, turn the heat down and
keep it simmering gently for 20–25 minutes or until the rice
is tender and dry.

FRENCH RICE SALAD

SERVE WITH GRILLED BEEF OR CHICKEN.

1½ PINTS (900ML)
BOILING WATER

8 FL OZ (225ML) LONG
GRAIN WHITE RICE

SALT

1 TEASPOON SAFFRON
POWDER

1 PINT (450G) FRESH
MUSSELS

3 OZ (75G) BLACK
OLIVES, PITTED AND
HALVED

1 SMALL ONION,
CHOPPED

1 SMALL RED PEPPER,
CHOPPED

1 SMALL GREEN PEPPER,
CHOPPED

1 SMALL YELLOW
PEPPER, CHOPPED

4 MEDIUM TOMATOES,
PEELED AND CHOPPED

DRESSING:

1 CLOVE GARLIC,
CRUSHED

1 EGG YOLK

6 TABLESPOONS OLIVE
OIL

1½ TABLESPOONS CIDER
VINEGAR

1 TABLESPOON PERNOD

SALT AND BLACK
PEPPER

SERVES 4–5

Start by pouring the boiling water on to the rice. Add salt and saffron. Bring to the boil, then lower the heat and cook the rice gently until just tender. Drain well, rinse in cool water and put aside.

While the rice is cooking, wash the mussels and discard those which are open. Place the cleaned mussels in a pan with plenty of water and bring to the boil. Cover and simmer for 10–12 minutes. Drain and discard the unopened ones. Remove the mussels from their shells, leaving some in the shell for garnishing.

Prepare the dressing: place the garlic and egg yolk in a bowl and whisk. Then start adding the olive oil slowly, whisking all the time. When all the oil has been added, add the vinegar, Pernod, salt and pepper. Now pour the dressing on to the rice, mixing it carefully. Add the olives, mussels, chopped onion, peppers and tomatoes. Garnish with the mussels in their shells.

TROPICAL RICE SALAD

INGREDIENTS

An exotic salad for hot summer days.

8 FL OZ (225ML) LONG GRAIN WHITE RICE

1 GRAPEFRUIT

1 OZ (25G) FLAKED ALMONDS

1 LARGE BANANA

JUICE OF 1 LEMON

2 OZ (50G) SULTANAS

5 SLICES FRESH OR CANNED PINEAPPLE

1 OZ (25G) PINE KERNELS

SALT AND PEPPER

OLIVE OIL

SERVES 4

Start by cooking the rice in plenty of salted boiling water until just tender. Rinse under cold water, drain well and set aside.

Peel the grapefruit, taking care to cut deep round inside the skin. Loosen the sections of grapefruit from the core and remove the membrane and pips. Blanch the almonds for 4 minutes. Dice the banana and sprinkle it with lemon juice. Mix the rice carefully with the fruits, almonds, sultanas and pine kernels. Dress the salad with olive oil, salt and pepper.

BROWN RICE SALAD

INGREDIENTS

8 FL OZ (225ML) BROWN RICE

15 OZ (425G) CAN CHICK PEAS, DRAINED

1 STICK CELERY, CHOPPED

3 OZ (75G) PINE KERNELS

4 OZ (125G) SULTANAS

1 SMALL RED PEPPER, DICED

SALT AND BLACK PEPPER

SERVES 4–5

First cook the rice in plenty of boiling salted water until it is just tender. Drain, rinse in cold water and drain again. Set aside. Combine chick peas with the rest of the ingredients. Mix well, add the rice and serve on a bed of lettuce.

RICE WITH WILD RICE

THE CONTRASTING COLOURS OF THE TWO TYPES OF RICE AND THEIR DIFFERENT FLAVOURS MAKE THIS DISH DELICIOUS. YOU CAN SERVE IT WITH GAME.

SERVES 4–5

Start by heating the butter in a saucepan and fry the onion for 1–2 minutes. Add the ham and the rice, stirring so that they are well coated with the butter, then add the stock. Cover with a lid, bring to the boil and then lower the heat. Cook the rice very gently for about 15 minutes or until it is tender and dry.

In another pan cook the wild rice in plenty of salted boiling water until just tender (about 15–20 minutes), then drain it. Warm the cognac and add it to the white rice, forking it to separate the grains.

Pile the white rice in a large serving dish and arrange the wild rice around it.

INGREDIENTS

2 OZ (50G) BUTTER

1 MEDIUM ONION, CHOPPED

2 OZ (50G) HAM, DICED

8 FL OZ (225ML) LONG GRAIN WHITE RICE

16 FL OZ (450ML) CHICKEN STOCK

4 FL OZ (125ML) WILD RICE

1 FL OZ (25ML) COGNAC

SEPHARDI JEWISH RICE

INGREDIENTS

1 TABLESPOON CHICKEN FAT

1 MEDIUM ONION, CHOPPED

3 KOSHERED CHICKEN LIVERS, CUT INTO SLICES

3½ OZ (100G) MUSHROOMS, CHOPPED

8 FL OZ (225ML) PATNA RICE

16 FL OZ (450ML) CHICKEN STOCK

1 CLOVE GARLIC, CRUSHED

1 TABLESPOON TOMATO PUREE

1 TEASPOON PAPRIKA

SALT AND BLACK PEPPER TO TASTE

I AM PARTICULARLY PLEASED TO INCLUDE THIS JEWISH RECIPE FROM LONG AGO, WHEN PICKING OVER THE RICE BEFORE PASSOVER WAS A TRADITIONAL TASK OF THE JEWISH HOUSEWIFE. THE METHOD USED FOR COOKING THE RICE IS THE ONE USED BY SEPHARDI COOKS.

SERVES 4

Heat the chicken fat in a cast iron casserole. Add the onion and fry until soft. Add the chicken livers and stir around for a few minutes before adding the mushrooms. Add the rice and cook for 5 minutes. Now add half the stock, stir once, cover and let it simmer gently until the rice has absorbed the liquid. Add the rest of the stock, the garlic, tomato purée and seasonings.

Cover and place in a pre-heated oven 350F/180C/Gas 4 for 20 minutes or until the rice is tender and dry. Serve immediately.

RICE WITH NUTS

INGREDIENTS

2 OZ (50G) BUTTER

2 CLOVES GARLIC, CRUSHED

1 OZ (25G) WALNUTS, ROUGHLY CHOPPED

1 OZ (25G) HAZEL NUTS, ROUGHLY CHOPPED

1 OZ (25G) FLAKED ALMONDS

8 FL OZ (225ML) BROWN RICE

16 FL OZ (450ML) CHICKEN STOCK

SALT TO TASTE

1 TABLESPOON FRESH CHOPPED PARSLEY

SERVES 4

Heat the butter in a saucepan and fry the garlic and nuts. Add the rice and stir for 1 minute, then add the chicken stock and salt. Cover with a lid and bring to the boil. Lower the heat and cook the rice very gently for 25–30 minutes. Spoon the rice on to a large serving dish and sprinkle with parsley.

ENGLISH KEDGEREE

INGREDIENTS

8 FL OZ (225ML) WHITE RICE

16 FL OZ (450ML) BOILING FISH STOCK

1 LB (450G) SMOKED POACHED HADDOCK FILLETS

PEPPER

NUTMEG

JUICE OF HALF A LEMON

5 FL OZ (150ML) SINGLE CREAM

2 OZ (50G) BUTTER

3 HARD-BOILED EGGS, CHOPPED

SERVES 4

Cook the rice by pouring the boiling fish stock on to it. Add salt, cover and cook gently for 15 minutes. Meanwhile, take the skin and the bones from the haddock and flake it. Now add pepper, nutmeg and lemon juice to the cream. Mix the rice carefully with the butter, cream, chopped eggs and flaked haddock. Serve immediately.

INDIAN YOGHURT RICE

INGREDIENTS

You can serve this rice with any meat dish.

2 TABLESPOONS OIL

1 MEDIUM ONION, CHOPPED

1 CLOVE GARLIC, CRUSHED

2 TEASPOONS CURRY POWDER

5 FL OZ (150ML) BROWN RICE

10 FL OZ (275ML) VEGETABLE STOCK, MADE WITH 1 LARGE

SERVES 2

Heat the oil and soften the onion and garlic in it. Add the curry powder and rice. Stir for 2 minutes, then add the stock, salt to taste, wine and turmeric. Bring to the boil, then lower the heat, cover and simmer for approximately 40 minutes. Stir in the yoghurt and coriander before serving.

CARROT, 3 STICKS CELERY, PARSLEY AND A BAY LEAF

SALT

4 TABLESPOONS DRY WHITE WINE

PINCH TURMERIC

8 OZ (225G) PLAIN YOGHURT

1 TEASPOON FRESH CORIANDER

GARDENER'S RICE

INGREDIENTS

Colourful, tasty and easy to make, this rice dish is really inviting.

½ OZ (10G) BUTTER

1 SMALL ONION, CHOPPED

5 FL OZ (150ML) LONG GRAIN WHITE RICE

10 FL OZ (275ML) BOILING WATER

SERVES 2

Start by heating the butter; soften the onion in it, then add the rice and stir so that it is well coated with the butter. Now add the remaining ingredients. Stir once, cover with a lid and when it starts to boil, lower the heat and let it simmer very gently without stirring for about 15 minutes.

3 OZ (75G) GREEN PEAS (FRESH SHELLED)

2 MEDIUM CARROTS, DICED SMALL

3 OZ (75G) SWEETCORN (FROZEN OR TINNED)

2 OZ (50G) SULTANAS

½ RED PEPPER, DICED

GREEN RICE

INGREDIENTS SERVE WITH ANY MEAT DISH.

2 OZ (50G) BUTTER

1 MEDIUM ONION, CHOPPED

2 OZ (50G) BACON, DICED

8 FL OZ (225ML) LONG GRAIN WHITE RICE

16 FL OZ (450ML) CHICKEN STOCK

SALT AND PEPPER

18 OZ (500G) FRESH SPINACH LEAVES WITHOUT STALKS

1 TABLESPOON CHOPPED PARSLEY

2 OZ (50G) PARMESAN CHEESE, GRATED

SERVES 4

Heat the butter in a saucepan and fry the onion for 1 minute. Add the bacon and fry it for another minute, then add the rice and stir to get it well coated with the butter. Now add the stock and salt and pepper and bring to boiling point. Cover with a lid and lower the heat.

Next blanch the spinach leaves in boiling water for 3 minutes and chop them finely. Add to the rice, stir once and let it simmer until dry and tender. Add the parsley and Parmesan cheese and serve immediately.

GERMAN RICE

2 OZ (50G) BUTTER

1 MEDIUM ONION, CHOPPED

8 FL OZ (225ML) LONG GRAIN WHITE RICE

½ PINT (275ML) PALE ALE AT ROOM TEMPERATURE

8 FL OZ (225ML) BOILING CHICKEN STOCK

SALT AND BLACK PEPPER

2 OZ (50G) PARMESAN CHEESE, GRATED

9 OZ (250G) EXTRAWURST (GERMAN SAUSAGE), SLICED

THIS GERMAN RICE IS FULL OF FLAVOUR AND HAS A DELICIOUS AROMA.

SERVES 4

Heat the butter in a saucepan and fry the onion for 1 minute. Then add the rice and stir to get it well coated with the butter. Next add the beer, stir and bring to the boil, allowing the rice to draw the flavour from the beer. After 5 minutes, add the boiling stock, salt and pepper. Stir and cover with a lid. Lower the heat and let the rice cook very gently.

Add the Parmesan and the sliced sausage 5 minutes before the end of the cooking time. Stir, cover again and cook until the rice is tender and dry. Serve immediately.

RICE AU GRATIN

A FRAGRANT AND CRISPY RICE DISH THAT CAN BE SERVED WITH BAKED TOMATOES AND RED PEPPERS.

SERVES 4

First cook the rice by pouring the stock on to the rice. Add salt and saffron. Cover with a lid, bring to boiling point and then lower the heat and let the rice cook very gently until tender and dry.

While the rice is cooking, prepare the sauce. Heat 2oz (50g) of the butter in a saucepan and add the flour, stirring it for 1–2 minutes, then add the milk gradually, stirring all the time to avoid lumps. Lower the heat and continue stirring for about 3 minutes. Add salt, pepper and nutmeg.

Remove from the heat and add the 2 egg yolks. Now mix the sauce with the rice and add the Parmesan cheese and the rest of the butter. Beat the egg whites to soft peaks and gently fold into the rice mixture. Spoon the rice into a greased mould and bake in a pre-heated oven 375F/190C/Gas 5 for 30 minutes or until the rice is light golden. Serve immediately.

INGREDIENTS

8 FL OZ (225ML) LONG GRAIN WHITE RICE

16 FL OZ (450ML) CHICKEN STOCK

SALT

1 TEASPOON SAFFRON POWDER

3 OZ (75G) BUTTER

1 OZ (25G) FLOUR

½ PINT (275ML) MILK

PEPPER

¼ TEASPOON NUTMEG, FRESHLY GRATED

2 EGGS, SEPARATED

3 OZ (75G) PARMESAN CHEESE, GRATED

GREEK DOLMADES

INGREDIENTS

3 OZ (75G) BUTTER

1 MEDIUM ONION, CHOPPED

4 FL OZ (125ML) WHITE RICE

2 PINTS (1.1 LITRES) BEEF STOCK

SALT AND PEPPER

1 LB (450G) MINCED LAMB

1 DESSERT SPOON CHOPPED PARSLEY

1 TEASPOON DRIED OREGANO

1 TEASPOON DRIED ROSEMARY

12 OR 14 VINE LEAVES, FRESH OR TINNED

2 TEASPOONS LEMON JUICE

8 OZ (225G) GREEK YOGHURT

THIS IS A TYPICAL GREEK DISH AND MAY BE SERVED WITH A JUG OF GREEK YOGHURT.

SERVES 4–5

Start by heating 1 oz (25g) of the butter in a saucepan and fry the onion for 1 minute. Add the rice and stir for another minute. Pour 8 fl oz (225ml) of the stock on to the rice. Add salt, cover with a lid and bring to the boil. Then lower the heat and cook the rice gently until tender and dry. Meanwhile mix the lamb with the parsley, oregano and rosemary. Add salt and pepper and mix well. Stir in the rice and set aside.

Blanch the fresh vine leaves for 5 minutes or, if using tinned ones, wash and dry them carefully. Place 1½ spoonfuls of the rice and lamb mixture on each leaf. Fold them to make small neat parcels or dolmades.

Place them closely in a casserole, pour over the rest of the stock and the lemon juice and dot with the rest of the butter. Put a heavy plate on top to keep the dolmades covered with the stock. Cover with a lid and cook very gently on top of the stove for 45–50 minutes. Lift the dolmades from the stock with a large perforated spoon and serve them with a bowl of Greek yoghurt.

MEXICAN RICE

THIS RICE DISH HAS THE PUNGENCY CHARACTERISTIC OF MEXICAN DISHES. THE CHILLI CERTAINLY GIVES IT A KICK.

INGREDIENTS

OIL FOR FRYING

1 MEDIUM ONION, CHOPPED

1 RED CHILLI, DESEEDED AND FINELY CHOPPED

8 FL OZ (225ML) LONG GRAIN WHITE RICE

16 FL OZ (450ML) CHICKEN STOCK

3 OZ (75G) SWEETCORN, TINNED OR FROZEN

1 LARGE CARROT, DICED SMALL

SALT

SERVES 4

Heat 3 tablespoons of oil in a saucepan and fry the onion and chilli. Stir for 1 minute. Add the rice and stir for another minute. Add the chicken stock, sweetcorn, carrot and salt. Cover with a lid and bring to the boil. Lower the heat and cook very gently for 15 minutes, or until it is tender and dry. Serve at once.

RICE SLICES

THESE SLICES OF RICE CAN BE SERVED WITH COLD MEAT AND SALAD DURING SUMMER DAYS.

INGREDIENTS

8 FL OZ (225ML) LONG GRAIN WHITE RICE

4 OZ (125G) PICKLED VEGETABLES

1 OZ (25G) GREEN OLIVES, SEEDED, CUT INTO RINGS

½ OZ (15G) POWDERED GELATINE

2 OZ (50G) MAYONNAISE

SALT AND PEPPER

2 OZ (50G) DOUBLE CREAM

SERVES 4

Start by cooking the rice in plenty of slightly salted water until just tender. Drain and put aside.

Chop the pickled vegetables and add to the rice. Add the olives and stir. Dissolve the gelatine in 6 tablespoons of hot water and stir until completely dissolved. Add the rice and mayonnaise. Mix well, adding salt and pepper to taste. Then whip the double cream and fold it into the rice mixture.

Spoon it into a mould 7 inches by 3 inches (18cm by 7.5cm) approximately and refrigerate it for 2–3 hours. Just before serving, dip the mould in hot water for 4–5 seconds. Place a serving dish over the mould and turn it upside down. Cut the rice into slices and serve immediately.

RING OF RICE

INGREDIENTS

2 OZ (50G) BUTTER

1 MEDIUM ONION, CHOPPED

9 FL OZ (250ML) WHITE LONG GRAIN RICE

2 FL OZ (50ML) DRY WHITE WINE

16 FL OZ (450ML) CHICKEN STOCK

1 TEASPOON CURRY POWDER

6 OZ (175G) SHELLED AND COOKED PRAWNS

6 TABLESPOONS TOMATO KETCHUP

4 OZ (125G) MAYONNAISE

1 TEASPOON WORCESTERSHIRE SAUCE

FEW DROPS CHILLI SAUCE

1 TABLESPOON LEMON JUICE

SALT

PARSLEY FOR GARNISHING

SERVES 4

First heat the butter in a saucepan and sauté the onion. Add the rice and stir to coat it with the butter. Add the wine and cook for 2 minutes. Add the stock and the curry powder. Stir once, cover with a lid and bring to the boil. Lower the heat and cook the rice very gently for 15 minutes or until it is tender and dry.

While the rice is cooking, prepare the prawns. Blend the tomato ketchup with the mayonnaise. Add the Worcestershire sauce, chilli sauce, lemon juice and salt. Taste, correct the seasoning if necessary and mix the prawns into the sauce.

Spoon the rice into a ring mould, pressing it well down. Then place a serving dish over the mould and turn it upside down. Fill the centre of the ring with the prawns and garnish with parsley.

RICE WITH ASPARAGUS

---

2 OZ (50G) BUTTER

1 MEDIUM ONION, CHOPPED

12 HEADS ASPARAGUS, CUT IN HALF

SALT AND PEPPER

10 FL OZ (275ML) LONG GRAIN WHITE RICE

THE SMOKY TASTE OF ASPARAGUS GIVES THIS RICE DISH A LOVELY, UNUSUAL FLAVOUR.

SERVES 6

Heat the butter in a saucepan and fry the onion for 1–2 minutes. Add the asparagus with a dash of salt and pepper and stir around. Add the rice and stir for 1 minute. Add the chicken stock and a little more salt. Cover with a lid and bring to the boil. Lower the heat and cook the rice very gently for 15 minutes. Add the cream and parsley and serve at once.

1 PINT (570ML) CHICKEN STOCK

4 OZ (125G) DOUBLE CREAM

1 TABLESPOON CHOPPED PARSLEY

BROWN RICE WITH HERBS

INGREDIENTS

---

2 OZ (50G) BUTTER

1 MEDIUM ONION, CHOPPED

1 CLOVE GARLIC, CRUSHED

½ TABLESPOON PARSLEY, CHOPPED

THE LOVELY FLAVOUR OF THIS RICE MAY VERY WELL COME FROM YOUR OWN GARDEN. IT IS THE AROMA AND TASTE OF FRESH HERBS THAT MAKES IT UNIQUE.

SERVES 4

Heat the butter in a saucepan and sauté the onion and garlic. Add the herbs and stir for 1–2 minutes. Add the rice and stir to get it well coated. Add the stock and salt, cover with a lid and bring to the boil. Lower the heat and cook the rice gently for 25–30 minutes. Discard the rosemary and marjoram and serve immediately.

1 SPRIG ROSEMARY

1 SPRIG MARJORAM

8 FL OZ (225ML) BROWN RICE

16 FL OZ (450ML) CHICKEN STOCK

SALT

NESTS OF RICE

1½ OZ (40G) BUTTER

1 MEDIUM ONION, CHOPPED

8 FL OZ (225ML) LONG GRAIN WHITE RICE

16 FL OZ (450ML) CHICKEN STOCK

2 OZ (50G) PARMESAN CHEESE, GRATED

2 OZ (50G) DOUBLE CREAM

4 LARGE EGGS

SALT AND PEPPER

Excellent as a light meal accompanied by a green salad.

SERVES 4

Heat 1 oz (25g) of the butter in a saucepan and sauté the onion. Add the rice and stir it around so that it is well coated with the butter. Add the stock and cook the rice very gently for 15 minutes or until it is tender and dry. Add the Parmesan and the double cream and mix well.

Spoon the rice into an 8 inch (20.5cm) round baking dish. Make 4 nests in the rice and break an egg into each. Season the eggs with salt and pepper. Put ¼ teaspoon of butter over each egg. Bake in a pre-heated oven 350F/180C/Gas 4 until the eggs have just set. Serve at once.

MALAYSIAN GINGER RICE

INGREDIENTS

10 FL OZ (275ML) BOILING CHICKEN STOCK

5 FL OZ (150ML) WHITE SHORT GRAIN RICE

1 TABLESPOON GRATED FRESH GINGER

SALT

Malaysian cookery does not always deliver a hot bite, more often it is a titillation for palates seeking the adventure of wonderful spices.

SERVES 2

Start by pouring the boiling stock on to the rice. Add the

ginger and salt and stir once. Cover and cook very gently for about 15 minutes. When the rice is cooked, spoon it into a mould. Cover with buttered foil and press it down with any weight you have at hand.

Stand the rice overnight. Then cut it into squares, cover and re-heat in the oven for 12–15 minutes.

FRIED RICE WITH ARTICHOKES

INGREDIENTS

1 FL OZ (25ML) OLIVE OIL

1 MEDIUM ONION, CHOPPED

1 CLOVE GARLIC, CRUSHED

1 SMALL GREEN CHILLI, SEEDED AND FINELY CHOPPED

1 RASHER BACON WITHOUT RIND, FINELY CHOPPED

SERVES 6

Heat the oil in a saucepan and fry the onion, garlic and chilli for 2 minutes. Add the bacon and fry for 1 more minute before adding the rice. Stir around and then add the wine. Mix all the ingredients carefully. Add the stock and salt. Cover with a lid and bring to the boil. Lower the heat and cook the rice very gently for 15 minutes.

Cut the artichokes in half and add them 5 minutes before the end of cooking time. Stir once, cover and continue cooking.

When the rice is done, heat the butter in a large frying pan and fry it, stirring to keep all the grains separate. Fry for 2 minutes and serve at once. Garnish with the parsley.

10 FL OZ (275ML) LONG GRAIN WHITE RICE

3 FL OZ (75ML) DRY WHITE WINE

1 PINT (570ML) CHICKEN STOCK

SALT

14 OZ (400G) TIN ARTICHOKE HEARTS

1 OZ (25G) BUTTER

1 TABLESPOON CHOPPED PARSLEY

CHINESE RICE BALLS

INGREDIENTS

THESE ORIENTAL RICE BALLS ARE VERY NICE WITH GREEN SALAD.

6 FL OZ (175ML) WHITE RICE

8 DRIED MUSHROOMS, WELL WASHED

8 OZ (225G) MINCED PORK

1 TIN BAMBOO SHOOTS, DRAINED AND FINELY CHOPPED

1 TABLESPOON SOY SAUCE

1 TABLESPOON RICE WINE OR MEDIUM DRY SHERRY

1 TEASPOON GRATED FRESH GINGER

2 SHALLOTS OR 3 SPRING ONIONS, FINELY CHOPPED

1 CLOVE GARLIC, CRUSHED

2 EGG WHITES

SERVES 4

Cover the rice with cold water and stand for 3 hours. Drain and leave in a sieve for 30 minutes. Put the mushrooms in boiling water and leave for 30 minutes. Drain and chop them finely. Combine the pork with the bamboo shoots, mushrooms, soy sauce, wine or sherry, ginger, shallots or spring onions, garlic and egg whites.

Mix well and make balls using 2 teaspoons of the mixture at a time. Then roll the balls in the rice to cover them completely. Place the balls in a steamer, separating one from the other. Cover and steam for 15 minutes. Serve with soy sauce as a dip.

CHINESE PINEAPPLE RICE

CHINESE EMIGRANTS HAVE FORMED LARGE COMMUNITIES IN ALMOST ALL COUNTRIES OF THE WORLD AND HAVE INTRODUCED THEIR WAY OF COOKING AND THEIR EXOTIC DISHES EVERYWHERE. AT THE SAME TIME THEY HAVE INCORPORATED NEW INGREDIENTS INTO THEIR CUISINE; THOSE OF THEIR ADOPTED COUNTRIES. SUCH IS THE CASE OF THE PINEAPPLE, FOR EXAMPLE, THAT THEY FOUND IN MALAYSIA, INDONESIA, THE CARIBBEAN AND IN OTHER TROPICAL COUNTRIES.

SERVES 2

Start by pouring the boiling water on to the rice. Add the salt and bring to the boil. Then lower the heat, cover and simmer for about 15 minutes. Set aside.

Cut the pineapple in half lengthways; taking out the flesh without breaking the outer shell; dice the flesh.

Mix the shallots, chestnuts, pepper, soy sauce, curry powder, pineapple and rice. Spoon the mixture into the two pineapple shells. Cover with a double sheet of foil and bake for 10–12 minutes at 350F/180C/Gas 4. Sprinkle with almonds before serving.

INGREDIENTS

10 FL OZ (275ML) BOILING WATER

5 FL OZ (150ML) LONG GRAIN WHITE RICE

SALT

1 LARGE PINEAPPLE

3 SHALLOTS, CHOPPED

1 TIN WATER CHESTNUTS, DRAINED AND CHOPPED

1 RED PEPPER, DICED

2 TEASPOONS SOY SAUCE

1 TEASPOON CURRY POWDER

½ OZ (10G) TOASTED ALMONDS

CHINESE FRIED RICE

INGREDIENTS

THIS IS A LOVELY RICE DISH WITH AN ORIENTAL TASTE.

10 FL OZ (275ML) WATER

5 FL OZ (150ML) WHITE RICE

SALT

4 DRIED MUSHROOMS, WASHED

1½ TABLESPOONS SESAME OIL

1 CLOVE GARLIC, CRUSHED

½ TEASPOON GRATED FRESH GINGER

2 SHALLOTS, CHOPPED

1 MEDIUM RED PEPPER, DICED

1 TIN BABY CORN, SLICED

⅓ CUCUMBER, DICED

3½ OZ (100G) GREEN PEAS, SHELLED AND COOKED

1 TABLESPOON SOY SAUCE

SERVES 2

Bring the water to the boil. Add the rice and salt. Cover with a lid. Lower the heat and cook the rice very gently until tender and dry.

Cover the mushrooms with boiling water, stand for 20–30 minutes, then drain and chop them. Heat the oil in a wok, add garlic, ginger, shallots and pepper and stir for 1–2 minutes. Add mushrooms, corn, cucumber and peas and stir-fry for 2 minutes.

Pour in the soy sauce and rice. Stir for another 2 minutes and serve immediately.

RICE WITH SPARE RIBS

RICE WITH SPARE RIBS OR *ARROZ CON HUESITO* (RICE WITH SMALL BONES) IS A VENEZUELAN DISH THAT DATES BACK TO THE SECOND HALF OF THE LAST CENTURY. THE FIRST TIME IT WAS MENTIONED WAS IN POPULAR SONGS THAT EMERGED JUST AFTER THE LIBERATION OF THE SLAVES. SINCE THEN THIS DISH HAS BEEN ONE OF THE TRADITIONAL DISHES ENJOYED IN VENEZUELAN COOKERY. IT WAS PARTICULARLY TASTY IN THE DAYS BEFORE REFRIGERATION AND INTENSIVE FARMING. TODAY YOU HAVE TO SUPPLY THE LOST FLAVOUR WITH ADDED INGREDIENTS. STILL, IT CONTINUES TO BE A DELICIOUS RICE DISH.

SERVES 2–3

Begin by heating half the cooking oil in a frying pan; fry the spare ribs on both sides to a golden brown colour and put them in a casserole. Now add the remaining oil to the pan, fry the onion and garlic for 3 minutes, then add the tomatoes and fry for 3 more minutes, adding the wine and parsley. Pour the contents of the frying pan on to the spare ribs.

Add the rice, salt and boiling water. Stir once, put on a lid and bring the casserole to boiling point. Then lower the heat and let it simmer very gently without stirring for approximately 40 minutes.

INGREDIENTS

4 TABLESPOONS COOKING OIL

8 SPARE RIBS, CUT IN HALVES

1 ONION, CHOPPED

2 CLOVES GARLIC, CRUSHED

4 TOMATOES, PEELED AND CHOPPED

3 TABLESPOONS RED WINE

1 TABLESPOON FRESH CHOPPED PARSLEY

5 FL OZ (150ML) BROWN RICE

SALT

10 FL OZ (275ML) BOILING WATER

JAPANESE SUSHI

INGREDIENTS

8 FL OZ (225ML) SHORT GRAIN RICE

15 FL OZ (400ML) BOILING WATER

SALT

3 TABLESPOONS APPLE VINEGAR

2 TABLESPOONS SAKE

1 TABLESPOON SUGAR

5 SHEETS NORI, TOASTED

1 SMALL BAMBOO MAT

Japanese cuisine is one of the most delicate and refined in the world. Its fans of cucumber, butterflies of strawberries and roses of tomatoes and oranges delight the eye and anticipate the pleasure of the dish. Sushi is one of the many Japanese dishes which have a new and intriguing taste.

SERVES 4–5

Start by covering the rice with cold water and stand for 1 hour. Drain well and then pour boiling water on to the rice. Add salt, cover and bring to the boil, then reduce the heat and keep it simmering gently until it is tender and dry. Remove from heat and stir in the vinegar, sake and sugar. Allow the rice to cool slightly.

Meanwhile prepare the omelette for the filling. Heat the oil in a frying pan. Add the sugar, salt and water to the beaten eggs. When the oil is hot, pour half the mixture into the frying pan and lower the heat a little. Cook until the edges of the omelette begin to dry out. Remove from the heat and

FILLING

COOKING OIL

2 TEASPOONS SUGAR

SALT

1 TABLESPOON WATER

2 LARGE EGGS, BEATEN

1 SMALL CUCUMBER, PEELED

3½ OZ (100G) HAM

2 TEASPOONS WASABI PASTE OR HORSERADISH

3 OR 4 LARGE SPINACH LEAVES

2½ OZ (60G) SLICED PICKLED GINGER

carefully turn it over. Return to the heat and cook the other side for about 30 seconds. Remove from the heat and put aside. Cook the other half of the egg mixture in the same way. Using a sharp knife, cut the omelettes and the ham into strips. Cut the cucumber vertically into long strips.

Now cut a strip about 1½ inches (4cm) wide from each nori leaf. Place the large piece of nori in the centre of the bamboo mat and place the narrow strip of nori in the centre. This helps to strengthen the nori during the rolling.

Next spread about a fifth of the rice over the nori leaf, leaving an edge of approximately 1 inch (2.5cm). Make a furrow in the centre of the rice; if it is too sticky, moisten your fingers with water and vinegar. Spread Wasabi paste or horseradish along the hollow centre of the rice, then place a strip of ham on top of it, a strip or two of omelette followed by a strip of spinach leaf, cucumber and some pickled ginger.

Use the bamboo mat to help roll the sushi, pressing as you roll. Remove the bamboo mat and with a sharp knife, cut the sushi into slices of 1½ inches (4cm). Repeat this process with all nori sheets until all are used up.

BIRYANI

A FRAGRANT AND EXQUISITE RICE, SERVED IN INDIA ON SPECIAL OCCASIONS.

8 FL OZ (225ML) BASMATI RICE

SALT

OIL FOR FRYING

18 OZ (500G) LAMB, CUT INTO CUBES

2 LARGE ONIONS, CUT INTO RINGS

3 CLOVES GARLIC, CRUSHED

2 OZ (50G) FRESH GINGER, PEELED AND GRATED

½ TEASPOON GROUND CARDAMOM SEEDS

½ TEASPOON GROUND CINNAMON

½ TEASPOON GROUND CORIANDER

2 APPLES, PEELED, DESEEDED AND CUT INTO SLICES

1 TEASPOON SAFFRON POWDER

1 OZ (25G) FLAKED AND TOASTED ALMONDS

1 OZ (25G) WALNUTS, ROUGHLY CHOPPED

1 OZ (25G) HAZEL NUTS, ROUGHLY CHOPPED

2 TABLESPOONS ROSE WATER

½ TEASPOON FRESHLY GROUND NUTMEG

½ TEASPOON GROUND CUMIN

½ TEASPOON GROUND BLACK PEPPERCORNS

5 GROUND WHOLE CLOVES

1 OZ (25G) GROUND ALMONDS

8 OZ (225G) PLAIN YOGHURT

8 FL OZ (225ML) WATER

BUTTER

1 OZ (25G) SULTANAS

1 OZ (25G) RAISINS

SERVES 5–6

Wash the rice five times and place in a colander to dry for 45 minutes. Heat the oil in a large saucepan, fry the lamb until golden brown and set aside. In the same oil, fry the onion rings until golden and set aside. Add a little more oil and fry the garlic, ginger and spices. Stir around for 1 minute, then return the lamb to the saucepan together with its juices. Stir so that the meat absorbs the flavours. Add the ground almonds and stir. Add the yoghurt 1 tablespoonful at a time, stirring to get it well blended with the sauce. Add the water, stir, cover with a lid and cook over a medium heat for about 1 hour.

While the lamb is cooking, heat 1 tablespoon of butter and toss the sultanas and raisins in it for a few seconds. Set aside. Add a little more butter, fry the apples until golden and set them aside. In a small saucepan heat 2 tablespoons of butter and fry the saffron. Set this coloured butter aside. Now bring to the boil 3 pints (1.75 litres) of salted water, cook the rice for 5–6 minutes only and drain.

Place the lamb and its sauce in a baking dish that can be taken to the table. Pile the rice on top of the lamb and trickle the saffron butter over it. Place the onions and apples around the rice and scatter the nuts, sultanas and raisins over it. Cover the dish with foil and bake in a pre-heated oven 325F/170C/Gas 3 for 2½ hours. Before serving, sprinkle the rose water over the Biryani for a delicious exotic touch.

NASI GORENG

THIS IS A DELICIOUS INDONESIAN RICE, A COMPLETE MEAL ON ITS OWN.

INGREDIENTS

10 FL OZ (275ML) BOILING FISH STOCK

5 FL OZ (150ML) WHITE RICE

SALT

4 TABLESPOONS COOKING OIL

3 EGGS, LIGHTLY BEATEN

1 SMALL ONION, CHOPPED

2 CLOVES GARLIC, CRUSHED

5 OZ (150G) SHELLED PRAWNS

½ CUCUMBER, CHOPPED

3½ OZ (100G) BEAN SPROUTS

½ TEASPOON CHILLI POWDER

1 TABLESPOON SOY SAUCE

SERVES 4

Start by pouring the boiling fish stock on to the rice. Add salt, cover and bring to the boil. Lower the heat and cook gently for 15 minutes. Keep warm.

Next heat 2 tablespoons of oil in a frying pan and fry the eggs to make an omelette. Cut it into strips. Heat the remaining oil in a saucepan or wok and fry the onion and garlic until soft. Add the prawns, cucumber and bean sprouts and stir for 1–2 minutes. Add the chilli powder, rice and soy sauce. Stir once more and garnish with the omelette strips before serving.

BANGKOK RICE WITH CHICKEN

INGREDIENTS

1 FRESH CHICKEN, 2½-3 LBS (1-1.4KG)

3 ONIONS

3 TABLESPOONS COOKING OIL

1 BAY LEAF

SALT

1 SPRIG PARSLEY

10 FL OZ (275ML) WHITE RICE

2 TABLESPOONS PEANUT BUTTER

½ TABLESPOON CHILLI POWDER

1 TEASPOON GROUND CORIANDER

1 CLOVE GARLIC, CRUSHED

1 TEASPOON GROUND CUMIN

PINCH GROUND MACE

4 OZ (125G) SHELLED PRAWNS

4 OZ (125G) DICED HAM

GARNISH:

½ CUCUMBER, SLICED

2 HARD-BOILED EGGS, QUARTERED

12 COOKED PRAWNS IN THEIR SHELLS

THAI AND MALAYSIAN WAYS OF COOKING HAVE BEEN INFLUENCED BY INDIA'S. THEY HAVE IN COMMON THE ART OF BLENDING SPICES AND HERBS WHICH ORIGINATES MORE THAN 6000 YEARS AGO. THE BLENDING OF SPICES AND MIXING OF HERBS ARE ONE OF THE COOK'S DAILY TASKS. HENCE THE FRESHNESS, PUNGENT AROMA AND SHARP TASTE FOUND IN MANY ORIENTAL DISHES. THIS DELICIOUS RICE FROM BANGKOK IS A SAMPLE OF THAI CUISINE AND MAKES A MEAL ON ITS OWN. YOU CAN, AS THEY DO IN THAILAND, ACCOMPANY IT WITH FRESH FRUITS AND VEGETABLES.

SERVES 6

Place the chicken in a pan with 2 pints (1.1 litres) of water. Add 1 onion, bay leaf, salt and parsley. Cook for 45 minutes or until tender. Measure the stock to 1 pint (570ml). Place this stock in a saucepan, add the rice and salt and bring to the boil. Lower the heat, cover and cook the rice very gently. Put aside.

While the rice is cooking, remove the skin from the chicken and cut the meat into small pieces. Peel and slice 2 onions and fry them until golden. Add the peanut butter, chilli, coriander, garlic, cumin, mace, prawns, ham and chicken. Fry for approximately 6 minutes. Add the rice and cook for

another 4 minutes. Serve garnished with slices of cucumber, quarters of hard-boiled eggs and cooked, unpeeled prawns.

If you wish, arrange small side dishes with apricot, slices of tomato dressed with sugar and lemon, slices of orange, green and red pepper and fried sliced bananas with lemon juice.

INDIAN LEMON AND COCONUT RICE

SERVE WITH LAMB OR CHICKEN STEW.

INGREDIENTS

PLENTY OF BOILING WATER

8 FL OZ (225ML) WHITE RICE

SALT

½ TEASPOON TURMERIC

1 OZ (25G) BUTTER

1 MEDIUM ONION, FINELY CHOPPED

½ TEASPOON MUSTARD SEEDS

½ TEASPOON CHILLI POWDER

1 TEASPOON COARSELY GRATED LEMON RIND

2 CLOVES GARLIC, CHOPPED

4 FL OZ (125ML) TINNED COCONUT MILK

2 TABLESPOONS LEMON JUICE

4 OZ (125G) SHREDDED COCONUT

SERVES 4

Pour the boiling water on to the rice. Add salt and turmeric. Cook for 8 minutes, then rinse the rice under cold water and drain it well.

Next heat the butter in a large pan, add the onion and cook until light brown. Add the mustard seeds and chilli powder. Stir for a minute, add the rice and stir to get it well coated. Now add the lemon rind, garlic, coconut milk and lemon juice. Bring to the boil and then reduce the heat. Cover the pan and cook gently until the rice is tender.

Place the shredded coconut on an oven tray and toast it in a moderate oven for about 3–4 minutes. Sprinkle the coconut on top of the rice before serving.

RICE POT FROM HUNZA

1 OZ (25G) BUTTER

1 MEDIUM ONION, CHOPPED

1 CLOVE GARLIC, CRUSHED

1 SPRIG FRESH ROSEMARY

3 OZ (75G) CASHEW NUTS, ROUGHLY CHOPPED

4 FL OZ (125ML) BROWN RICE

4 FL OZ (125ML) BUCKWHEAT

16 FL OZ (450ML) CHICKEN STOCK

SALT

THIS RICE DISH COMES FROM HUNZA, THE LAND OF SHANGRI-LA WHERE LONGEVITY AND HEALTH ARE FAMOUS. THE FIRST TIME I TASTED IT WAS IN MALAKA (MALAYSIA) IN A RESTAURANT WHOSE CHEF WAS A HUNZAKUT. THE RICE WAS SERVED IN SMALL ROUND BOWLS TO ACCOMPANY CHICKEN IN A HOT SAUCE. DUALAT, THE CHEF, SAID THAT IN FORMER TIMES, WHENEVER SOMEONE SET OUT ON A JOURNEY IN HIS COUNTRY, IT WAS CUSTOMARY TO TAKE WITH HIM A SMALL SACK OF BUCKWHEAT, RICE, SOME APRICOTS AND A CAN OF WATER. HE WOULD COOK HIS POT ON AN OPEN FIRE. THE RICE I HAD JUST EATEN WAS A VERSION OF THAT COMMON HUNZAKUT DISH. DUALAT GLADLY GAVE ME THE RECIPE.

SERVES 4–6

Heat the butter in a saucepan and fry the onion and the garlic. Stir for 1 minute. Add the rosemary, cashew nuts, rice and buckwheat. Stir around for 1–2 minutes more and then add the stock and salt. Cover with a lid and bring to the boil. Lower the heat and cook gently for 25–30 minutes.

You can serve this pot with tomato sauce if you wish.

RICE WITH TUNA FISH

INGREDIENTS

This unusual rice dish scattered with stuffed peaches comes from Indonesia.

16 FL OZ (450ML) CHICKEN STOCK

8 FL OZ (225ML) WHITE RICE

SALT

7 OZ (200G) TIN OF TUNA

3 HEAPED TABLESPOONS MAYONNAISE

1 TABLESPOON TOMATO KETCHUP

1 TEASPOON WORCESTERSHIRE SAUCE

2 SPRING ONIONS

PEPPER

14 OZ (400G) TIN PEACH HALVES (UNSWEETENED)

PARSLEY FOR GARNISHING

SERVES 4

Bring the chicken stock to the boil and add the rice and salt. Cover with a lid, lower the heat and cook the rice gently for 15 minutes.

While the rice is cooking, flake the tuna and mix with the mayonnaise, tomato ketchup and Worcestershire sauce. Wash and trim the spring onions, chop them and add to the tuna mixture with salt and pepper to taste.

Rinse the peach halves, pat dry with kitchen paper and fill them with the tuna mixture. Place the rice in a large serving dish and make hollows in it to accommodate the stuffed peaches. Serve garnished with parsley.

INDIAN BASMATI RICE

This is the most delicate, aromatic and delicious Indian rice dish. It can be served with any meat or even eaten on its own.

5 FL OZ (150ML) BASMATI
RICE

2 TABLESPOONS
COOKING OIL

1 MEDIUM ONION,
CHOPPED

SERVES 2

Wash the rice 5 or 6 times until you see the water running clear. Now place the rice in a sieve to dry for half an hour. Heat the oil in a saucepan and fry the onion and garlic. Add the garam masala, chilli powder and rice. Stir it to get the rice well coated. Now pour the boiling stock on to the rice; stir once, cover and bring to the boil. Lower the heat and let it simmer gently for 12–15 minutes.

2 CLOVES GARLIC,
CRUSHED

1 LEVEL TEASPOON
GARAM MASALA

PINCH CHILLI POWDER

10 FL OZ (275ML)
BOILING CHICKEN
STOCK

PARCELS OF RICE

THE ANDEAN PEOPLE WHO LIVE UP IN THE MOUNTAINS PROTECT THEMSELVES FROM THE ICY WINDS OF THE PARAMOS NOT ONLY WITH THICK CLOTHING BUT ALSO BY HAVING NUTRITIOUS MEALS. PARCELS OF RICE OR *NINOS ENVUELTOS* AS THIS DISH IS CALLED IN THE VENEZUELAN ANDES IS A TYPICAL REGIONAL RICE DISH AND IS BOTH TASTY AND SATISFYING. IT IS SUPPOSED THAT THE NAME *NINOS ENVUELTOS* MEANING WRAPPED CHILDREN, COMES FROM THE WAY WOMEN FROM THOSE ALTITUDES WRAP THEIR BABIES, LIKE PARCELS, TO PROTECT THEM FROM

THE COLD WHILE TRAVELLING AROUND OR WORKING IN
THE FIELDS.

SERVES 4

Start by pouring the boiling water on to the rice and as soon
as it starts to boil again, lower the heat and let it simmer
gently until the rice is tender and dry. Put aside and let it cool
a little.

Wash the cabbage leaves and blanch them in boiling water
for 5 minutes. Rinse the leaves in cool water and dry them
carefully with kitchen paper. Put aside and prepare the filling.

Heat the oil and soften the onion and garlic in it, then add
the cumin and minced pork, stirring all the time. Add half the
tomatoes and the red pepper and let it simmer. Cook for
about 15–20 minutes and then add the raisins and parsley.

Heat the oven to 350F/180C/Gas 4. Mix the rice with the
cooked pork; place a heaped tablespoon of the rice mixture
in each leaf and fold it to make a neat parcel. Place the
stuffed leaves in a baking tin side by side. When all the leaves
are filled, pour over the remaining tomatoes. Cover and bake
for 30 minutes.

10 FL OZ (275ML)
BOILING WATER

5 FL OZ (150ML) LONG
GRAIN WHITE RICE

SALT

12 TENDER LEAVES OF
SPRING CABBAGE

COOKING OIL

1 ONION, CHOPPED

2 CLOVES GARLIC,
CRUSHED

PINCH CUMIN

8 OZ (225G) MINCED
PORK

1½ LBS (700G)
TOMATOES, PEELED AND
CHOPPED

½ RED PEPPER, DICED

2 TABLESPOONS
RAISINS

½ TABLESPOON
CHOPPED PARSLEY

VENEZUELAN CONGEE

INGREDIENTS

4 OZ (125G) BLACK BEANS

10 FL OZ (275ML) BOILING WATER

2 TABLESPOONS OLIVE OIL

1 SMALL ONION, CHOPPED

2 CLOVES GARLIC, CRUSHED

¼ TEASPOON GROUND CUMIN

1 SMALL GREEN OR RED PEPPER, CHOPPED

SALT

1 OZ (25G) BUTTER

5 FL OZ (150ML) LONG GRAIN RICE

2 PINTS (1.1 LITRES) BOILING WATER

CHOPPED PARSLEY, TO GARNISH

Rice and black beans are for Venezuelans what fish and chips are for the English. Because it was nutritious, satisfying and cheap, it used to be the daily dish of the poor, and frequently the leftovers were served for breakfast the following day. As far as I know, Congee or *congri* as some people say in Caracas, has been prepared in Venezuela for a century or more.

In Venezuela and other Latin American countries, beans do not usually need soaking before cooking as they are fresher than in other countries. Cooking times may vary between 1 and 2 hours, depending on the age of the beans. If you suspect the beans may be stale, it is advisable to soak them overnight in cold water with a teaspoon of bicarbonate of soda. Rinse the beans before cooking them in fresh water. You may, if you wish, replace the black beans with aduki beans which are more tender and do not take so long to cook.

SERVES 2

Place the beans in a saucepan with the water, cover with a lid and bring to the boil. Then lower the heat and cook the beans until tender. Heat the olive oil in a frying pan and add the onion, garlic and cumin. Fry for 1 minute and then add the pepper. Cook for another 1–2 minutes and pour on to the beans. Add a pinch of salt and continue cooking until the cooking liquid has doubled in consistency. Adjust the seasoning.

While the beans are cooking, pour the boiling water on to the rice. Add salt and bring back to boiling point. Then lower the heat and cook the rice very gently for 15 minutes or until tender and dry. Put aside and let it cool.

By this time the beans must be almost dry and thick. Heat the butter and stir in the beans, frying for 1–2 minutes. Then add the rice. Mix everything, stirring for 2 more minutes and serve at once with a teaspoon of chopped parsley on top if you wish.

PABELLON

INGREDIENTS

1 LB (450G) BEEF SKIRT

2 MEDIUM ONIONS

1 CARROT, CUT INTO
CHUNKS

2 STICKS CELERY, CUT
INTO PIECES

1 BAY LEAF

SMALL BUNCH PARSLEY

8 FL OZ (225ML) LONG
GRAIN WHITE RICE

OIL FOR FRYING

1 CLOVE GARLIC,
CRUSHED

4 LARGE TOMATOES,
PEELED AND CHOPPED

SALT

SERVES 4

First place the meat in a pan with enough water to cover. Add one of the onions, the carrot, celery, bay leaf and parsley. Cover the pan and bring to the boil. Lower the heat and cook until the meat is tender (about 1½ hours). If the cooking liquid has been reduced, add a little more water and continue cooking. When it is done, lift the meat from the broth and set aside. Strain the stock and measure it to get 16 fl oz (450ml).

Place the stock in a saucepan with a teaspoon of salt. Bring to the boil and add the rice. Cover with a lid and lower the heat. Cook the rice very gently for 15 minutes.

While the rice is cooking flake the meat. Heat 4 tablespoons of oil in a large frying pan and fry the garlic and the remaining onion, finely chopped. Fry for 2 more minutes and add the meat. Stir and fry for a few more minutes. Add the tomatoes and salt to taste. Stir for 3–4 minutes. Tip the meat and its sauce on to the rice and mix well.

You can serve Pabellon with fried black beans and plantains as it is usually served in Venezuela. For the black beans, see Venezuelan Congee (page 52). When the beans are cooked, fry them in olive oil. For the fried plantains, see Rice with Plantains (page 55).

PABELLON IS A VENEZUELAN DISH AS TRADITIONAL AS CONGEE (PAGE 52). WHEN FRIED PLANTAINS ARE ADDED, THE DISH IS CALLED *PABELLON CON BARANDA* (PABELLON WITH RAILS) BECAUSE THE SLICES OF PLANTAIN ARE PLACED AROUND THE RICE, MEAT AND BEANS, ENCLOSING IT ALL.

RICE WITH PLANTAIN

This rice, which is a Colombian dish, can also be found in towns on the west coast of Venezuela, on the border with Colombia where plantain is in abundance. There the cheese they use is a variety called *Queso Amarillo* (yellow cheese) and white rice instead of brown. You can, if you wish, use white rice, but you will take away the slightly nutty flavour of the brown rice and the beneficial fibre content.

SERVES 6

Bring the stock to the boil and add the rice and salt. Cover with a lid, lower the heat and cook the rice very gently for 25–30 minutes or until it is tender and dry. Add the butter and set aside.

Peel the plantains and cut them in half, then cut each half into 4 slices. Heat the oil in a frying pan and fry the plantain slices in batches until golden brown. Pour the rum on to the slices and sprinkle with sugar.

Now mix the eggs with the rice and place a layer of this mixture in a buttered baking mould. Place a layer of fried plantain slices on top and sprinkle with cheese. Add another layer of rice, plantain and cheese and finish with rice. Dot with butter and place the mould in a pre-heated oven 350F/180C/Gas 4 for 25 minutes or until golden. Serve at once.

INGREDIENTS

1 PINT (570ML) CHICKEN STOCK

10 FL OZ (275ML) BROWN RICE

SALT

2 LARGE OR 3 MEDIUM PLANTAINS

OIL FOR FRYING

3 FL OZ (75ML) RUM

1 TEASPOON SUGAR

3 EGGS, BEATEN

1 OZ (25G) BUTTER

4 OZ (125G) GRATED CHEDDAR CHEESE

RICE WITH MARROW BONES

INGREDIENTS

2 LBS (900G) MARROW BONES FROM OX SHOULDER AND THIGH

2 SMALL CARROTS, PEELED AND SLICED

2 MEDIUM ONIONS

1 BAY LEAF

1 STICK CELERY

2 SPRIGS OF THYME

2 OZ (50G) BUTTER

4 FL OZ (125ML) DRY WHITE WINE

8 FL OZ (225ML) LONG GRAIN WHITE RICE

½ TEASPOON SAFFRON POWDER

SALT

1 OZ (25G) PARMESAN CHEESE, GRATED

SERVES 4

Place the ox bones in a pan, covered with water and bring to the boil. Add the carrots, 1 onion, the bay leaf, celery and thyme. Cover the saucepan with a lid, lower the heat and cook for 1 hour. Lift out the bones and with a pointed teaspoon, extract the marrow and place it in a dish. Strain the court bouillon and measure 16 fl oz (450ml) making up the amount with water if necessary. Discard the vegetables.

Heat the butter. Chop the remaining onion and fry it for 1–2 minutes. Add the marrow bone and the wine, stir and cook for 2 minutes. Add the rice and stir it around for another minute. Add the saffron, the court bouillon and salt. Stir once. Cover with a lid and bring to the boil. Lower the heat and simmer gently for 15 minutes or until the rice is tender and dry. Add the Parmesan and fork the rice to separate the grains. Serve at once.

THIS IS A FAMILY RECIPE. MY MOTHER USED TO PREPARE IT WHEN WE WERE YOUNG CHILDREN AND WE ENJOYED IT VERY MUCH. BUTCHER'S SHOPS IN VENEZUELA USED TO SELL MEAT AND BONES MIXED OR SEPARATELY AS THE CUSTOMERS WISHED. IT WAS NOT DIFFICULT THEN TO GET ENOUGH MARROW BONE TO PREPARE THE RICE. I MYSELF COOKED THIS DISH IN CARACAS YEARS AGO AND MY CHILDREN ALSO ENJOYED THE DELICATE FLAVOUR AND THE CREAMY TEXTURE THE MARROW IMPARTS TO THE DISH.

RICE WITH CALZONES

INGREDIENTS

1 OZ (25G) BUTTER

2 MEDIUM ONIONS

8 FL OZ (225ML) WHITE RICE

1 TEASPOON SAFFRON POWDER

16 FL OZ (450ML) CHICKEN STOCK

3 TABLESPOONS OLIVE OIL

1 LB (450G) PORK SHOULDER, CUT INTO CUBES

2 CLOVES GARLIC, CRUSHED

1 TABLESPOON FLOUR

3 FL OZ (75ML) RED WINE

4 TOMATOES, PEELED AND CHOPPED

1 SMALL GREEN PEPPER, SEEDED AND CHOPPED

1 TEASPOON OREGANO

SALT AND PEPPER

2 OZ (50G) OLIVES, SEEDED AND CUT INTO RINGS

I GOT THIS RECIPE FROM A SPANISH COOK SOME YEARS AGO. THIS DISH AND *CABRITO ASADO* (ROAST SUCKLING GOAT) WERE HER SPECIALITIES. THE DISH IS RICH, FULL OF FLAVOUR AND A COMPLETE MEAL ON ITS OWN.

SERVES 4

Heat the butter in a saucepan and sauté 1 onion, finely chopped. Add the rice and stir it around for 1 minute. Add the saffron and the chicken stock. Cover with a lid and bring to the boil. Lower the heat and cook the rice very gently for 15 minutes.

While the rice is cooking, prepare the pork. Heat the olive oil in a pan and fry the pork until golden brown. Remove the pork and in the same oil fry the other onion, chopped, and the crushed garlic. Return the pork to the pan and sprinkle the flour on it, stirring around. Add the wine, tomatoes, green pepper, oregano, salt and pepper. Cover the pan and place in a pre-heated oven 350F/180C/Gas 4 for 30–35 minutes. Add the olive rings 10 minutes before the end of cooking time.

Spoon the rice on to a large serving dish and fill the centre with the pork stew. Serve immediately.

BAKED RICE WITH SARDINES

INGREDIENTS

THIS DISH COMES FROM SPAIN WITH ITS INVITING SMELL OF SARDINES COOKED IN WHITE WINE.

8 FL OZ (225ML) BROWN RICE

16 FL OZ (450ML) FISH STOCK

OLIVE OIL

1 MEDIUM ONION, CHOPPED

1 CLOVE GARLIC, CRUSHED

14 OZ (400G) FRESH SARDINES, CLEANED AND WITH HEAD OFF

2 FL OZ (50ML) DRY WHITE WINE

2 TABLESPOONS CHOPPED PARSLEY

SALT AND PEPPER

SERVES 4

Bring the fish stock to the boil. Add the rice and a teaspoon of salt. Cover with a lid, lower the heat and cook for about 30 minutes. Add 2 tablespoons of olive oil and set aside.

Heat 3 tablespoons of olive oil and sauté the onion and the garlic. Add the sardines, seasoned with salt and pepper. Fry them for 3 minutes, then add the wine and cook for a further 3–4 minutes. Mix the rice with the parsley, add the sardines and their juices and stir carefully. Spoon the mixture into a baking dish and place in a pre-heated oven 350F/180C/Gas 4 for about 20 minutes. Serve at once.

PHILIPPINE RICE

PHILIPPINE COOKERY HAS A STRONG SPANISH INFLUENCE FROM COLONIAL DAYS. THERE IS A PHILIPPINE PAELLA SIMILAR TO THE COSTA BRAVA'S. THIS RICE WITH ITS SAFFRON, PICKLES AND ALMONDS SPEAKS LOUDLY OF PAST SPANISH DAYS.

SERVES 2-3

Begin by adding the rice, cardamom, cinnamon, saffron and salt to the boiling water. Stir once, cover and cook gently for approximately 15 minutes or until the rice is tender and dry.

Now heat the oil in a wok or large saucepan and fry the almonds until lightly browned. Put aside, then add the rice to the wok and stir a little. Add the pickles, bean sprouts and red pepper. Stir once more and fry for 1-2 minutes. Add the almonds and serve immediately.

INGREDIENTS

5 FL OZ (150ML) WHITE RICE

10 FL OZ (275ML) BOILING WATER

⅓ TEASPOON GROUND CARDAMOM

⅓ TEASPOON GROUND CINNAMON

⅓ TEASPOON SAFFRON POWDER

SALT

1 TABLESPOON SESAME OIL

1 OZ (25G) SLIVERED ALMONDS

1 TABLESPOON MIXED PICKLES, CHOPPED

3½ OZ (100G) BEAN SPROUTS

1 SMALL RED PEPPER, CHOPPED

SPANISH PAELLA

INGREDIENTS

1 3 LB (1.4KG) CHICKEN

SALT AND BLACK PEPPER

1 BUNCH PARSLEY

2 BAY LEAVES

1 SPRIG MARJORAM

OREGANO

OLIVE OIL

1 MEDIUM ONION, CHOPPED

12 FL OZ (350ML) LONG GRAIN WHITE RICE

1 LB (450G) RIPE TOMATOES, FINELY CHOPPED

2 RED PEPPERS, SLICED

8 OZ (225G) GREEN PEAS

8 OZ (225G) LARGE SHELLED PRAWNS, PLUS 8 LARGE COOKED PRAWNS IN THEIR SHELLS TO GARNISH

1 LB (450G) MUSSELS, CLEANED

½ TEASPOON POWDERED SAFFRON

6 OZ (175G) SPANISH CHORIZO, SLICED

THIS IS THE KING OF THE SPANISH RICE DISHES, FULL OF FLAVOUR AND A COMPLETE MEAL ON ITS OWN.

SERVES 6

Start by preparing the chicken stock. Separate the wings, legs and breast from the chicken and put the carcass and giblets in a large pan. Cover with water and bring to the boil. Season with salt and pepper and add the parsley, bay leaves, marjoram and oregano. Cook for 30 – 40 minutes, strain and set aside.

Next heat the oil in a heavy-based saucepan. Fry the chicken joints and the breast cut into 4 pieces, until golden brown, then set aside. Fry the onion in the same saucepan, stirring until soft. Add the rice and stir it round to get it well coated with the oil. Return the chicken to the pan and add the vegetables, mussels and peeled prawns.

Measure the chicken stock and pour 1½ pints (900ml) on to the rice mixture. Add the saffron powder. Stir once and cover with a lid. Bring to the boil and then lower the heat and cook it gently for about 15 – 20 minutes. Add the chorizo 8 minutes before the rice is done.

Serve in a large earthenware dish garnished with unshelled prawns.

BLACK RICE

THIS BLACK RICE MUST NOT BE CONFUSED WITH THE
SICILIAN BLACK RICE WHICH IS A DESSERT. OUR BLACK
RICE COMES FROM VENICE. I TASTED IT FOR THE FIRST
TIME SOME YEARS AGO IN A LOCAL TRATTORIA. LIKE MANY
TOWNS ON THE ADRIATIC COAST, VENICE BOASTS RICE
WITH FISH DISHES, AND AMONG THEM IS THIS BLACK RICE
WHICH WILL PLEASE ALL SEA FOOD LOVERS.

SERVES 4

First prepare and clean the squid. Pull the head and all the
innards out of the body. Cut off the tentacles. Discard head
and innards. Wash the ink sac carefully and place it in a pan
with a little boiling water. Press the sac to extract the ink and
set aside. Remove the transparent bone and the skin from the
body and tentacles and cut the squid into small pieces.

Heat the butter and fry the onion and garlic for 1–2
minutes. Add the parsley and the squid slices and stir for
another 2 minutes. Add the wine and the rice, stir and let the
rice absorb the flavours. Then add the fish stock and bring to
the boil. Cover with a lid and lower the heat. Let the rice
simmer for about 8 minutes before you strain the squid ink
and add it to the rice together with the salt and pepper. Stir
once, cover again and let it cook gently until the rice is tender
and dry. Serve at once with wedges of lemon.

INGREDIENTS

14 OZ (400G) SQUID

2 OZ (50G) BUTTER

1 ONION, CHOPPED

2 CLOVES GARLIC,
CRUSHED

1 TABLESPOON
CHOPPED PARSLEY

4 FL OZ (125ML) DRY
WHITE WINE

10 FL OZ (275ML) WHITE
LONG GRAIN RICE

1 PINT (570ML) FISH
STOCK

SALT AND PEPPER

1 LEMON, TO SERVE

PUMPKIN RISOTTO

INGREDIENTS

2 OZ (50G) BUTTER

3 SHALLOTS, FINELY CHOPPED

18 OZ (950G) PUMPKIN, SKINNED, SEEDED AND CUT INTO CUBES

8 FL OZ (225ML) ARBORIO RICE

SALT AND PEPPER

1 PINT (570ML) BOILING CHICKEN STOCK

GRATED RIND AND JUICE OF 2 ORANGES

1 TABLESPOON CHOPPED FRESH GINGER

8 FL OZ (225ML) SINGLE CREAM

RICE IS TO NORTHERN ITALY WHAT PASTA IS TO THE SOUTH. PUMPKIN RISOTTO IS AVAILABLE THERE FROM MID-SUMMER TO OCTOBER WHEN PUMPKINS ARE IN THE MARKET. I THINK IT MAKES A DELICIOUS FIRST COURSE FOR THE MICHAELMAS SEASON.

SERVES 4

Start by heating the butter in a saucepan. Add the shallots and stir around for 1–2 minutes. Add the pumpkin and the rice, salt and pepper. Stir for about 4 minutes, then start adding the chicken stock, 5 fl oz (150ml) at a time. Stir, lower the heat and leave the rice to cook gently.

Add the rind and orange juice and then the ginger. Keep adding the stock until the rice is tender and has absorbed it all. About 5 minutes before finishing the cooking, add the cream. Serve hot.

OLD TIMBALE OF RICE

A RICE DISH FROM LAZIO AND CAMPANIA. RICE DISHES FROM THESE AREAS ARE NOT CREAMY AND VELVETY LIKE THE RISOTTO FROM THE NORTH OF ITALY: THEY ARE DRY, FULL OF FLAVOUR AND BECAUSE OF THE INGREDIENTS,

MANY OF THEM ARE A MEAL ON THEIR OWN. TO THIS TYPE BELONGS OLD TIMBALE OF RICE. IT COMES FROM ROME AND IS BELIEVED TO HAVE BEEN PREPARED SINCE THE BEGINNING OF THE CENTURY. THIS DISH CAN BE SERVED AS A MAIN COURSE WITH A GREEN SALAD.

INGREDIENTS

3 OZ (75G) BUTTER

1 MEDIUM ONION, FINELY CHOPPED

8 FL OZ (225ML) SHORT GRAIN RICE

16 FL OZ (425ML) BOILING CHICKEN STOCK

1 OZ (25G) DRIED MUSHROOMS, WASHED

1 CLOVE GARLIC

2 TABLESPOONS DRY WHITE WINE

4 OZ (125G) CHUCK STEAK, MINCED

1 EGG, BEATEN

2 HARD-BOILED EGGS, CHOPPED

2 TABLESPOONS GRATED PARMESAN

5 OZ (150G) COTTAGE CHEESE OR RICOTTA

NUTMEG

SALT AND PEPPER

COOKING OIL

2 TABLESPOONS BREADCRUMBS

2 OZ (50G) WHITE BREAD WITHOUT THE CRUST, SOAKED IN A LITTLE MILK

SERVES 4

Start by heating 2 oz (50g) of the butter in a saucepan. Add the onion and stir for 2 minutes. Add the rice and stir to get it well coated with the butter. Next add the boiling chicken stock. Add salt, stir once, cover with a lid and cook gently for about 15–20 minutes.

Meanwhile soak the mushrooms for 20 minutes in tepid water. Then chop and fry them in the remaining butter. Add the garlic and stir for 2 minutes. Add the wine, lower the heat and let the mushrooms cook gently for a few minutes. Next mix the meat with the soaked bread, the egg, Parmesan cheese, nutmeg, salt and pepper; mix well.

Heat 3 tablespoons of oil in a frying pan and fry the meat mixture, stirring around to avoid it getting lumpy. Fry until the meat is lightly golden and put aside.

Now grease a round tin with a removable base and sprinkle with breadcrumbs. Tilt the tin to get it well covered. Use half the rice to cover the bottom and sides of the tin and then fill it with one layer of mushrooms; on top of this add a layer of chopped eggs, then a layer of cottage or Ricotta cheese and then a layer of meat. The last layer must be of rice. Bake the timbale for 15 minutes at 350F/180C/Gas 4. Serve hot in wedges.

RICE WITH QUAIL

INGREDIENTS

3 OZ (75G) BUTTER

2 MEDIUM ONIONS

8 FL OZ (225ML) WHITE RICE

16 FL OZ (450ML) CHICKEN STOCK

4 QUAILS, CLEANED

4 RASHERS OF BACON

JUICE AND RIND OF 2 LARGE ORANGES

SALT AND PEPPER

2 TABLESPOONS BRANDY

IN THE ITALIAN REGION OF VENETO IT IS SAID: 'IF VENETO HAD A COAT OF ARMS FOR ITS COOKERY, RICE WOULD BE ONE OF ITS SYMBOLS'. ONE OF THEIR SPECIALITIES IS RICE WITH QUAIL. ALTHOUGH RICE DISHES IN VENETO ARE ALMOST ALWAYS A FIRST COURSE, THIS CAN MAKE A LOVELY LUNCH ON ITS OWN.

SERVES 4

Heat 1 oz (25g) of the butter in a saucepan and fry one of the onions, chopped. Stir for 1 minute and then add the rice, stirring for another minute to get it coated with butter. Add the stock, cover the pan with a lid and bring to the boil. Lower the heat and cook the rice gently for 15 minutes.

While the rice is cooking, prepare the quails. Heat the rest of the butter in an ovenproof pan. Fry the remaining onion, chopped. Add the bacon and fry for 2 minutes, then add the quails and fry them until golden brown. Add the juice of the oranges, salt and pepper. Cover the pan with a lid and transfer to the oven 350F/180C/Gas 4. Cook for 40 minutes or until the quails are tender.

Place the quails in a dish and keep warm. Skim the excess fat from the cooking liquid and strain it. Reduce it a little by boiling it rapidly. Add the brandy and keep warm. Now spoon the rice into a large serving dish to form an 'x'. Place the quails in the angles and pour the sauce on to them. Garnish with strips of orange peel and serve at once.

RISOTTO FUME ALLA CHAMPAGNE

THIS EXQUISITE AND LUXURIOUS RISOTTO CAN BE SERVED AS A FIRST COURSE IN ANY SPECIAL DINNER.

SERVES 4

Start by heating 2 oz (50g) of the butter in a saucepan. Soften the onion in the butter, cooking it gently. Add the rice and stir to get it well coated with the butter. Add the salt and pepper and half the champagne. Stir until the rice has absorbed the champagne, then add the rest of the champagne and the stock. Stir and bring to the boil, then lower the heat and cook the rice gently for about 25 minutes.

Just before the end, add the cream and three-quarters of each of the cheeses, stirring gently until the rice is tender and creamy. Serve at once, dotted with the rest of the butter and the cheese.

INGREDIENTS

3 OZ (75G) BUTTER

1 MEDIUM ONION, FINELY CHOPPED

8 FL OZ (225ML) ARBORIO RICE

SALT AND PEPPER

5 FL OZ (150ML) CHAMPAGNE

1 PINT (570ML) BEEF STOCK

8 FL OZ (225ML) SINGLE CREAM

6 OZ (175G) SMOKED CHEESE (PROVOLONE), DICED

2 OZ (50G) FRESHLY GRATED PARMESAN CHEESE

65

RISOTTO WITH TRUFFLES

INGREDIENTS

3 OZ (75G) BUTTER

8 FL OZ (225ML)
ARBORIO RICE

3½ OZ (100G) TRUFFLES,
SLICED

1 PINT (570ML) BEEF
STOCK

6 OZ (175G) FRESHLY
GRATED PARMESAN
CHEESE

SALT AND PEPPER

IN RICE DISHES FROM THE ITALIAN VENETO, TRADITION AND IMAGINATION SEEM TO HAVE DECIDED THAT EVERY EDIBLE PLANT, ROOT, SEED, FUNGUS AND ANIMAL FROM SEA AND EARTH WILL END UP SOONER OR LATER IN A RISOTTO DISH. SO IT IS NOT SURPRISING TO FIND THIS EXQUISITE RISOTTO WITH TRUFFLES IN VENETO CUISINE. WHAT COULD BE SURPRISING IS THE PRICE OF ITS MAIN INGREDIENT: TRUFFLES. BUT THEN THEIR VALUE AND THEIR FLAVOUR HAVE BEEN RECOGNISED FROM LONG AGO. BESIDES, TRUFFLES HAVE THE MOST DELICIOUS AROMA. WHAT MAKES THEM SO EXPENSIVE IS THAT THEY ARE NOT HARVESTED BUT HUNTED BY USING SPECIALLY TRAINED DOGS AND PIGS. TRUFFLES GROW UNDERGROUND IN CALCAREOUS OAKWOODS. TRAINED DOGS AND PIGS CAN SMELL BURIED TRUFFLES FROM A LONG DISTANCE. IN ITALY, IN THE REGIONS OF EMILIA ROMAGNA, PIEMONTE AND TOSCANA, THE TRUFFLE HUNTING SEASON STARTS IN AUTUMN AND CAN LAST UNTIL FEBRUARY OR MARCH. THEN IS THE TIME FOR THE LUXURIOUS RISOTTO WITH TRUFFLES WHICH CAN BE SERVED AS A FIRST COURSE IN A DINNER OF FRESH SALMON OR YOUNG PHEASANT WITH APPLES.

SERVES 4

Heat the butter in a saucepan. Add the rice and stir to get it well coated with the butter. Add the truffles and the stock. Stir and bring to the boil. Then lower the heat and cook the rice gently for about 20–25 minutes until tender and creamy. Add the Parmesan cheese and serve at once.

RISOTTO ALLA FRAGOLA

A RISOTTO FROM PADOVA WHICH SHARES WITH THE REST OF THE VENETO REGION THE ART OF MAKING THE MOST DELICIOUS AND SURPRISING ITALIAN RISOTTOS. I WOULD SAY THAT THERE IS NOT A GRAIN THAT HAS STIRRED THE IMAGINATION OF NORTHERN ITALIAN CUISINE MORE THAN RICE. AS THEY SAY *LE PIATTI DI RISO SONO INFINITE* (RICE DISHES ARE INFINITE). THIS RISOTTO ALLA FRAGOLA IS A SUMMER TIME RISOTTO WHEN STRAWBERRIES ARE IN SEASON AND GIVE THE RICE NOT ONLY ITS FLAVOUR BUT ITS WONDERFUL PINK COLOUR.

INGREDIENTS

3 OZ (75G) BUTTER

1 MEDIUM ONION, FINELY CHOPPED

14 FL OZ (375ML) ARBORIO RICE

5 FL OZ (150ML) DRY WHITE WINE

SALT AND PEPPER

1½ PINTS (900ML) BOILING CHICKEN STOCK

1 LB (450G) STRAWBERRIES

8 FL OZ (225ML) SINGLE CREAM

6 OZ (175G) FRESHLY GRATED PARMESAN CHEESE

SERVES 6

Start by heating the butter in a large saucepan. Add the onion and soften it in the butter. Add the rice and stir so that it is well coated with the butter. Then add the wine, stir and lower the heat, allowing the rice to absorb it. Add the salt and pepper and start pouring the chicken stock on to the rice 5 fl oz (150ml) at a time and stirring occasionally.

Let it cook gently for about 25–30 minutes. Just before the end add half the strawberries puréed, the cream and half the cheese. Before serving, sprinkle with the remaining cheese and decorate with the rest of the strawberries.

Instead of strawberries you can use a melon, one half for the purée and the other half cut into cubes for the decoration.

ROMAN SUPPLI

8 FL OZ (225ML) WHITE RICE

16 FL OZ (450ML) BOILING WATER

SALT

COOKING OIL

1 MEDIUM ONION, CHOPPED

3½ OZ (100G) CHUCK STEAK, MINCED

1 STICK CELERY, FINELY CHOPPED

1 MEDIUM CARROT, PEELED AND GRATED

3 TOMATOES, PEELED AND CHOPPED

PEPPER

1 OZ (25G) PARMESAN CHEESE, GRATED

2 OZ (50G) SMOKED CHEESE, DICED SMALL

2 OZ (50G) MOZZARELLA, DICED SMALL

NUTMEG

1 EGG, BEATEN

1 OZ (25G) BREADCRUMBS

SUPPLI IS A ROMAN WORD FOR RICE CROQUETTE. IN ROME IT IS CALLED *SUPPLI AL TELEFONO* BECAUSE WHEN IT IS CUT HOT, THE MOZZARELLA CHEESE MAKES THREADS LIKE TANGLED TELEPHONE WIRES. SUPPLI MAKES A VERY GOOD LUNCH SERVED WITH A GREEN SALAD.

SERVES 4

Cook the rice by pouring the boiling water on to it. Add salt, cover with a lid and bring to the boil again. Then lower the heat and cook the rice gently until tender and dry. While the rice is cooking, heat 3 tablespoons of oil and fry the onion for 1 minute. Add the meat and stir around for 1–3 minutes, then add the celery, carrot, tomatoes, salt and pepper. Lower the heat and let it cook gently for 45 minutes, stirring from time to time.

Next mix the rice with the meat mixture and let it cool. Add the cheeses, nutmeg and beaten egg. Make this mixture into balls, using about 1½ tablespoons at a time.

When all the balls are made, roll them in breadcrumbs. Heat the oil and fry the balls in batches until golden brown. Serve immediately.

ARANCINI ALLA SICILIANA

This rice dish, originally from Sicily, can also be found in Puglia. It is a speciality of the south of Italy. The Arancini are in fact crisp and golden 'oranges' with a savoury filling.

SERVES 4–5

Bring 2 pints (1.1 litres) of salted water to the boil, add the rice and cook it until just tender. Drain, rinse in cool water and drain again.

While the rice is cooking, heat a tablespoon of oil and the butter and fry the onion; stir until it is soft. Add the peas and the meat, salt and pepper and stir for 1–2 minutes. Add the tomato sauce and the beef stock. Stir, let it cook gently for a few minutes and put aside.

Now place the rice in a bowl, add the cheese, 2 beaten eggs and pepper and mix well. Take one tablespoon of the rice mixture and make a ball with floured hands. Hollow the top with one finger and place a little of the meat mixture in it. Top with more rice and roll the ball round. Prepare the rest of the balls (arancini) in the same way.

Beat the remaining egg, dip each arancini in it and cover with breadcrumbs. Heat the oil and fry the arancini until golden brown. Drain on kitchen paper and keep hot. Before serving, garnish each arancini with a leaf of mint.

INGREDIENTS

8 FL OZ (225ML) ARBORIO RICE

COOKING OIL

1 OZ (25G) BUTTER

1 SMALL ONION, CHOPPED

8 OZ (225G) FRESHLY SHELLED GREEN PEAS

3½ OZ (100G) LEAN GROUND STEAK

SALT AND PEPPER

4 TABLESPOONS TOMATO SAUCE

2 TABLESPOONS BEEF STOCK

1½ OZ (40G) GRATED PARMESAN CHEESE

3 EGGS

4 OZ (125G) BREADCRUMBS

FRESH MINT LEAVES

RICE A LA MARINIERE

INGREDIENTS

3 TABLESPOONS OLIVE OIL

1 MEDIUM ONION, CHOPPED

1 MEDIUM GREEN PEPPER, DESEEDED AND CHOPPED

½ TEASPOON SAFFRON POWDER

8 FL OZ (225ML) WHITE RICE

4 TOMATOES, PEELED AND CHOPPED

DASH CHILLI SAUCE

4 OZ (125G) SHELLED PRAWNS

8 OZ (225G) MUSSELS, CLEANED

1 TIN SMOKED OYSTERS

SALT

16 FL OZ (450ML) FISH STOCK

SERVES 4

Heat the oil in a saucepan and fry the onion and green pepper. Add the saffron and the rice and stir to get the rice well coated. Add the tomatoes, chilli sauce, prawns, mussels and oysters. Mix well and add the salt and stock. Cover with a lid and bring to the boil. Lower the heat and cook very gently for 15 minutes. Serve with additional olive oil on top and crusty bread.

RISOTTO ALL'ISOLANA

A speciality of Isola delle Scalla, a town near Mantova in the Italian region of Lombardia. The Italian style and imagination in preparing rice are, in this particular dish, a revelation. A friend of mine said about this risotto: 'Taste it to believe it'.

SERVES 8

Rub the diced beef with salt and pepper and let it stand for 1 hour. Melt the butter in a pan and when it is hot, add the meat with the sprig of rosemary. Sear the meat well, then turn down the heat and finish cooking it, taking care that the meat does not become dry.

Next pour the boiling stock on to the rice. Add salt, bring to the boil, then lower the heat and cook the rice gently for about 30 minutes, stirring to prevent the rice from sticking. When cooked, it must be tender and creamy. Then remove the pan from the heat and stir in the meat and all the juices from the frying pan. Add the cheese with the cinnamon and serve immediately.

INGREDIENTS

11 OZ (300G) BEEF FILLET, DICED

SALT

BLACK PEPPER

7 OZ (200G) BUTTER

1 SPRIG ROSEMARY, WASHED

3 PINTS (1.75 LITRES) BOILING CHICKEN STOCK

2 LBS (900G) ARBORIO RICE

7 OZ (200G) STRONG CHEDDAR CHEESE, GRATED

1 TEASPOON GROUND CINNAMON

RICE WITH LOBSTER

A LAVISH RECIPE FOR SPECIAL OCCASIONS!

2 OZ (50G) BUTTER

2 SMALL ONIONS, CHOPPED

8 FL OZ (225ML) LONG GRAIN WHITE RICE

4 FL OZ (125ML) DRY WHITE WINE

16 FL OZ (450ML) CHICKEN STOCK

2 TABLESPOONS BRANDY

1 LB (450G) FRESHLY COOKED LOBSTER MEAT

SALT AND PEPPER

SERVES 4

Heat half the butter in a saucepan and sauté one of the chopped onions. Add the rice and stir for 1–2 minutes. Add the wine and stir to let the rice absorb the flavours. Cook for another minute, then add the stock. Cover with a lid and bring to the boil. Lower the heat and cook the rice gently for 15 minutes.

Meanwhile in another saucepan heat the rest of the butter and fry the other onion. Add the rest of the wine and the brandy. Stir for a few seconds and then add the lobster, salt and pepper. Stir and let it stand to absorb the flavours. Keep warm.

When the rice is ready, fold the lobster and its juices into the rice. Serve at once.

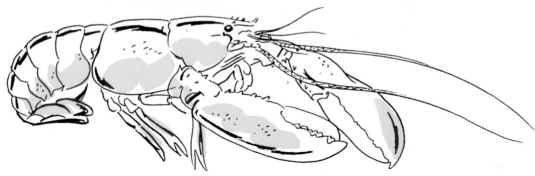

RICE QUICHE WITH CRABMEAT

10 FL OZ (275ML) CHICKEN STOCK

5 FL OZ (150ML) SHORT GRAIN RICE

SALT

1 OZ (25G) BUTTER

1 LARGE EGG

1 TABLESPOON FLOUR

1 TABLESPOON LEMON JUICE

THE LOVELY COMBINATION OF INGREDIENTS IN THIS QUICHE AND THE RICHNESS OF THE CRABMEAT MAKE THIS DISH THE CENTREPIECE OF A MEAL.

SERVES 4

First cook the rice. Bring the chicken stock to the boil and add the rice and salt. Cover with a lid, lower the heat and let it simmer gently for 15 minutes. Add the butter and set aside. Beat the egg with the flour, lemon juice and a little salt. Mix it with the rice. Now cover the base and sides of a quiche tin with the rice mixture. Place in a pre-heated oven 375F/190C/Gas 5 for 10 minutes, then set aside.

Meanwhile prepare the filling. Heat the butter in a saucepan and fry the onion until soft. Add the crabmeat and tomato purée and stir for 1 minute. Remove from the heat. Beat the eggs with the milk, salt and pepper in a bowl. Fold this mixture into the prepared crabmeat. Spoon this filling into the rice case and return to the oven. Bake until the filling is set and golden. Serve immediately.

FILLING

1 OZ (25G) BUTTER

1 ONION, FINELY CHOPPED

8 OZ (225G) FRESH OR FROZEN CRABMEAT, FLAKED

1 TABLESPOON TOMATO PUREE

3 EGGS

5 FL OZ (150ML) MILK

SALT AND PEPPER

RICE WITH RABBIT

INGREDIENTS

1 RABBIT, JOINTED

2 OZ (50G) BUTTER

1 ONION, CHOPPED

1 SPRIG THYME

1 BAY LEAF

1 TABLESPOON FLOUR

3 FL OZ (75ML) RED WINE

4 OZ (125G) MUSHROOMS, CHOPPED

4 TOMATOES, PEELED AND CHOPPED

SALT AND PEPPER

16 FL OZ (450ML) CHICKEN STOCK

8 FL OZ (225ML) BROWN RICE

PARSLEY FOR GARNISH

SERVES 4

Wash the rabbit joints and pat dry. Heat the butter in a saucepan and fry the rabbit until golden brown. Set the rabbit pieces aside and fry the onion in the same fat. Add the thyme, bay leaf and flour, stirring all the time. Return the rabbit to the saucepan together with any juices. Add the wine, mushrooms and tomatoes. Season with salt and pepper and cook over a medium heat for about 1 hour or until the rabbit is tender. Discard the thyme and the bay leaf.

While the rabbit is cooking, prepare the rice. Bring the stock to the boil and add the rice and salt. Cover with a lid, lower the heat and cook very gently for 25–30 minutes or until it is tender and dry. To serve, spoon the rice into a large serving dish and pile the rabbit stew in the centre. Garnish with parsley.

RICE WITH CHICKEN FRICASSEE

The combination of chicken with herbs and spices makes this a wonderful dish: creamy and full of flavour.

SERVES 4–5

Bring the chicken stock to the boil and add the rice and salt. Cover with a lid, lower the heat and cook the rice very gently for 15 minutes.

While the rice is cooking, cut the chicken breasts into small pieces and season with salt and pepper. Heat the butter in a saucepan and fry the chicken until golden brown. Set aside. Fry the onion and garlic in the same butter, then add the coriander and wine. Stir for a few seconds before returning the chicken to the pan. Lower the heat and cook gently for about 25–30 minutes.

Mix the two creams and season with lemon juice, tarragon, salt and pepper. Refrigerate for ½ hour. When the chicken is cooked, remove from the heat and add the mixed cream. Stir and add the rice, mixing well. Allow to stand for a few minutes before serving.

INGREDIENTS

- 16 FL OZ (450ML) CHICKEN STOCK
- 8 FL OZ (225ML) LONG GRAIN WHITE RICE
- SALT AND PEPPER
- 4 CHICKEN BREASTS
- 2 OZ (50G) BUTTER
- 1 SMALL ONION, CHOPPED
- 2 CLOVES GARLIC, CRUSHED
- ½ TABLESPOON FRESHLY GROUND CORIANDER
- 3 TABLESPOONS DRY WHITE WINE
- 4 FL OZ (125ML) DOUBLE CREAM
- 2 FL OZ (50ML) SOURED CREAM
- 1 TABLESPOON LEMON JUICE
- 2 TABLESPOONS CHOPPED TARRAGON

RICE WITH LAMB'S LIVER

INGREDIENTS

12 OZ (350G) LAMB'S LIVER, CUT INTO THIN SLICES

SALT AND PEPPER

¼ TEASPOON DRIED THYME

16 FL OZ (450ML) CHICKEN STOCK

8 FL OZ (225ML) LONG GRAIN WHITE RICE

3 TABLESPOONS OLIVE OIL

2 CLOVES GARLIC, CRUSHED

2 LARGE ONIONS, CUT INTO RINGS

4 FL OZ (125ML) APPLE JUICE

SERVES 4

Season the lamb's liver slices with salt, pepper and thyme and let them stand for ½ hour.

Boil the chicken stock and add the rice and salt. Cover with a lid and lower the heat. Cook the rice gently for 15 minutes.

Heat the oil in a saucepan and fry the garlic and onions. Add the liver slices and cook them over a moderate heat, turning them over once. When the liver is cooked, place it in a warm dish and cover with the onion rings.

To make the sauce, add the apple juice to the pan juices. Boil rapidly to reduce it by half. To serve, place the liver slices carefully on a large serving dish. Pour the apple sauce on top and spoon the rice around the liver to form a ring.

RICE CAKE WITH PARMA HAM

SERVES 4

Heat 1 oz (25g) of the butter in a saucepan and sauté half the garlic, crushed. Add the saffron and the rice and stir for 1–2 minutes. Add the wine and stir to let the rice absorb the flavours. When the wine has almost evaporated, add the stock and salt. Cover with a lid and bring to the boil. Lower the heat and cook the rice very gently for 15 minutes.

When the rice is cooking, heat the remaining 2 oz (50g) of butter and fry the remaining garlic and the onion. Stir for 1–2 minutes, add the mushrooms, salt and pepper and sprinkle in the flour, stirring all the time. Cook the mushrooms for a few minutes until you have a darkish sauce.

Next mix the rice with the beaten eggs, adding a pinch of salt if necessary. Now spoon half the rice into a buttered baking mould. Press down the rice with a tablespoon and spread the mushrooms on top. Place the Parma ham slices on top of the mushrooms and cover with the rest of the rice. Press down, dot with butter and bake in the oven 350F/180C/Gas 4 until golden. Let it stand for a few minutes and then turn carefully on to a serving dish. Serve in slices.

INGREDIENTS

3 OZ (75G) BUTTER

2 CLOVES GARLIC, CRUSHED

½ TEASPOON SAFFRON POWDER

8 FL OZ (225ML) WHITE RICE

3 FL OZ (75ML) DRY WHITE WINE

16 FL OZ (450ML) BEEF STOCK

SALT AND PEPPER

1 MEDIUM ONION, CHOPPED

3 OZ (75G) FLAT MUSHROOMS, FINELY CHOPPED

1 LEVEL TABLESPOON FLOUR

2 EGGS, BEATEN

3½ OZ (100G) PARMA HAM IN THIN SLICES

RICE WITH LEEKS

INGREDIENTS

16 FL OZ (450ML)
CHICKEN STOCK

8 FL OZ (225ML) LONG
GRAIN WHITE RICE

SALT AND PEPPER

1 LB (450G) LEEKS

2 OZ (50G) BUTTER

4 FL OZ (125ML) DRY
WHITE WINE

YOU WILL FIND THE SLIGHTLY SMOKY FLAVOUR OF LEEKS MIXED WITH RICE A SURPRISING AND PLEASANT COMBINATION. SERVE WITH FRESH TOMATO SAUCE IF YOU WISH.

SERVES 4

Bring the chicken stock to the boil and add the rice and salt. Stir once and cover with a lid. Lower the heat and cook the rice very gently for 15 minutes.

While the rice is cooking, trim the leeks, wash them well and chop them into about 1 inch (2.5cm) pieces. Heat the butter and fry the leeks seasoned with salt and pepper. Stir around for 2 minutes and then add the wine. Let the leeks cook gently, absorbing the flavours, until most of the wine has evaporated.

Set the leeks aside and keep them warm until the rice is cooked. Add the leeks and all their juices to the rice. Stir carefully and allow to stand for 1-2 minutes before serving.

RICE WITH CHESTNUTS

The unique taste of chestnuts gives this rice its distinct flavour. A rice for the season when leaves fall and fruits are ripe.

SERVES 6

Bring 18 fl oz (500ml) of the chicken stock to the boil, then add the rice and salt. Cover with a lid, lower the heat and cook very gently for 15 minutes.

Meanwhile heat the butter in an ovenproof saucepan, and fry the onion and celery. Add the chestnuts and stir around. Dissolve the cornflour in the sherry and add to the pan. Stir and gradually add the remaining chicken stock. Add salt and pepper and continue stirring until it starts to boil. Cover with a lid and transfer to a pre-heated oven 325F/170C/Gas 3 for 30 minutes or until the chestnuts are tender. Mix the rice with the chestnuts and serve at once.

IGREDIENTS

1½ PINTS (775ML) CHICKEN STOCK

9 FL OZ (250ML) LONG GRAIN WHITE RICE

SALT

2 OZ (50G) BUTTER

1 MEDIUM ONION, CHOPPED

1 CELERY STALK, CHOPPED

1 LB (450G) CHESTNUTS, PEELED

1 LEVEL TABLESPOON CORNFLOUR

2 FL OZ (50ML) MEDIUM DRY SHERRY

PEPPER

MOROCCAN RICE

INGREDIENTS

4 OZ (125G) BROWN LENTILS

8 FL OZ (225ML) WHITE RICE

2 OZ (50G) BUTTER, PLUS EXTRA FOR SERVING

1 SMALL ONION, CHOPPED

6 OZ (175G) MINCED LAMB

4 OZ (125G) DATES, STONED AND CHOPPED

½ TEASPOON SAFFRON POWDER

3 OZ (75G) SULTANAS

SALT AND PEPPER

4 TABLESPOONS WATER

SERVES 6

Start by cooking the lentils with a little salt in boiling water until tender. Drain and set aside. Cook the rice in plenty of boiling salted water until tender. Drain and set aside.

Heat the butter in a saucepan and add the onion. Stir until golden. Add the lamb and fry over a medium heat until brown. Add the dates, saffron and sultanas, salt and pepper and the water. Stir and cook gently for 10–12 minutes.

Now spread half the rice in a large serving dish and spread the lentils on top of it, followed by the meat and fruit mixture. Finish by spreading the remaining rice over. Reheat in a moderate oven for 15 minutes and serve with extra butter on top.

RICE AND PULSES HAVE BEEN MIXED TOGETHER FOR CENTURIES IN COUNTRIES AS FAR APART AS INDIA AND MOROCCO, TURKEY AND VENEZUELA. TRADERS, TRAVELLERS AND SOLDIERS INTRODUCED NEW DISHES AND EXCHANGED WAYS OF COOKING BETWEEN EAST AND WEST. IN THIS MOROCCAN RICE, THE ARAB INFLUENCE IS IN THE DRIED FRUITS WHICH GIVE THE DISH A TOUCH OF SWEETNESS, WHILE THE COMBINATION OF LENTILS, RICE AND LAMB MAKES IT A DELICIOUS AND SUBSTANTIAL MEAL.

ARMENIAN RICE

FROM THE EAST OF ARMENIA COMES THIS RICE DISH WHICH IS SERVED AT CHRISTMAS AND EASTER TIME. THE SITUATION OF ARMENIA, IN THE TRADING ROUTE BETWEEN EAST AND WEST, SUBJECTED IT TO THE INFLUENCE OF ARABS, TURKS, SYRIANS AND OTHER PEOPLES FROM THE MIDDLE EAST. THE FRUITS, NUTS AND SPICES IN MANY ARMENIAN DISHES ARE THE REMINDER OF THIS INFLUENCE, AND THIS RICE DISH IS RICH IN THEM. IT WAS A THRILLING EXPERIENCE THE FIRST TIME I TASTED THIS RICE AT A FRIEND'S HOME ON EPIPHANY DAY.

SERVES 6

Heat 2 oz (50g) of the butter and add the cinnamon and rice. Fry the rice, stirring round to get it well coated with the butter. Add the chicken stock and salt. Cover with a lid and bring to the boil. Lower the heat and cook the rice gently for 15 minutes or until it is tender and dry.

While the rice is cooking, place the orange juice in a small pan and bring to simmering point. Add the dried apricots, sultanas and raisins and cook them very gently for a few minutes. In a frying pan, brown the almonds slightly and put aside. Take one apple, wipe and core it. Put a little butter inside and place it in a small baking tin. Bake the apple in a pre-heated oven 350F/180C/Gas 4 for 10–15 minutes. Peel and slice the remaining apples and fry them in the rest of the butter. Set aside.

Now pile the rice in a large serving dish. Arrange the apple slices and apricots around the rice. Sprinkle the almonds, sultanas and raisins over the pile of rice and place the apple in a hollow on top. Fill the apple with brandy and set alight. It makes an impressive presentation.

INGREDIENTS

3 OZ (75G) BUTTER

1 TEASPOON GROUND CINNAMON

12 FL OZ (350ML) WHITE RICE

1½ PINTS (900ML) CHICKEN STOCK

1 TEASPOON SALT

4 FL OZ (125ML) ORANGE JUICE

4 OZ (125G) DRIED APRICOTS

3 OZ (75G) SULTANAS

3 OZ (75G) RAISINS

3 OZ (75G) FLAKED ALMONDS

4 APPLES

BRANDY

YUFKALI PILAFF

INGREDIENTS

4 CHICKEN BREASTS, SKINNED

3 LARGE CARROTS, DICED

4 CARDAMOM PODS

4 WHOLE CLOVES

SALT

3 OZ (75G) BUTTER

1 SMALL ONION, CHOPPED

9 FL OZ (250ML) LONG GRAIN WHITE RICE

4 OZ (125G) FROZEN PEAS

2 BEATEN EGGS MIXED WITH 1 TABLESPOON FLOUR

4 SHEETS FILO PASTRY

2 OZ (50G) PINE NUTS

2 OZ (50G) SULTANAS

PILAFFS FROM TURKEY AND OTHER MIDDLE EASTERN COUNTRIES ALWAYS INCLUDE FRUIT AND NUTS, BUT FEW ARE ENCASED IN PASTRY LIKE THIS ONE. THIS IS MY OWN VERSION OF THE YUFKALI PILAFF FROM ANKARA.

SERVES 6

First place the chicken in a saucepan with 1 pint (570ml) of water. Add the carrots, cardamom, cloves and salt and bring to the boil. Cover and cook over a medium heat until the chicken is tender and the stock has reduced a little. Take out the chicken and carrots; cut the chicken into chunks and put aside. Strain and measure the stock; you need 18 fl oz (500ml). If it is short, add water to complete the measure.

Heat 1 oz (25g) of the butter and fry the onion. Add the rice and stir for 1 minute. Add the stock, cover and bring to the boil. Lower the heat, cook the rice very gently for 15 minutes and set aside. Place the peas in a pan, add water and boil for 8–10 minutes. Drain and set aside.

Now mix the rice with the beaten eggs and flour. Line a 9 inch (23cm) baking tin with the 4 sheets of filo pastry, buttering each sheet generously. Spread a layer of rice over the pastry, followed by a mixture of chicken, peas, sultanas, pine nuts and carrots. Cover with another layer of rice and repeat as above, finishing with a layer of rice.

Fold the sheets of pastry over the filling to cover it

82

completely and brush the top with butter. Place in a pre-heated oven 375F/190C/Gas 5 for 30 minutes or until the dish is golden and crispy. Place a serving dish over the baking tin and turn it upside down. Serve immediately.

AMERICAN RICE AND FISH

INGREDIENTS

SERVES 4

Heat the butter in a saucepan and fry the onion. Add the rice and stir for 1 minute. Add the fish stock and salt. Cover with a lid and bring to the boil. Lower the heat and cook the rice gently for 15 minutes.

While the rice is cooking, poach the fish. Place it in a fish poaching kettle with the milk, bay leaf, salt, pepper and spices. Bring to simmering point and cook the fish for 10 minutes. Set aside and allow to cool in the poaching liquid.

Mix the rice with the green pepper, parsley, egg and Worcestershire sauce. Lift the fish from the cooking liquid, flake it and mix with the rice. Spoon the mixture into a baking tin and spread the breadcrumbs on top. Bake in a pre-heated oven 375F/190C/Gas 5 for 15 minutes. Serve at once.

1 OZ (25G) BUTTER

1 SMALL ONION, CHOPPED

8 FL OZ (225ML) PATNA RICE

16 FL OZ (450ML) FISH STOCK

SALT AND PEPPER

1 LB (450G) FRESH COD FILLETS

5 FL OZ (150ML) MILK

1 BAY LEAF

1 SMALL GREEN PEPPER, CHOPPED

3 CLOVES

5 WHOLE JAMAICA ALLSPICE

1 TABLESPOON CHOPPED PARSLEY

1 BEATEN EGG

1 TEASPOON WORCESTERSHIRE SAUCE

2 OZ (50G) BREADCRUMBS

RICE FROM TRINIDAD

INGREDIENTS

4 CHICKEN BREASTS,
CUT INTO PIECES

2 CLOVES GARLIC,
CRUSHED

1 TEASPOON MARJORAM

SALT AND BLACK
PEPPER

2 TABLESPOONS
WORCESTERSHIRE
SAUCE

2 TABLESPOONS
MUSCATEL WINE

3 TABLESPOONS OIL

1 TABLESPOON SUGAR

2 STICKS CELERY

1 LARGE ONION

4 FL OZ (125ML)
COCONUT MILK

1 6 OZ (175G) CAN
PIGEON PEAS

3 LARGE TOMATOES,
PEELED AND CHOPPED

1 RED CHILLI,
DESEEDED AND
CHOPPED

9 FL OZ (250ML) WHITE
RICE

15 FL OZ (400ML)
CHICKEN STOCK

2 OZ (50G) SULTANAS

2 OZ (50G) GREEN
OLIVES

Trinidad's cookery is part of Caribbean cuisine, where originally African influence and later that of Spain, England and France have left their trace. This exotic and tasty rice comes from Port of Spain.

SERVES 6

Place the chicken in a saucepan and season it with garlic, marjoram, salt, pepper and the Worcestershire sauce mixed with the Muscatel wine. Let it stand for 3 hours.

Heat the oil in a large saucepan. Add the sugar and when it starts to caramelise, add the chicken and fry, stirring around to get it golden brown. Chop the celery and onion and place them in a food processor. Add the coconut milk and make a purée. Pour this purée into a saucepan and add the pigeon peas. Stir and cook for about 10–12 minutes on a medium heat.

Now add the tomatoes and chilli to the chicken and cook for a few more minutes. Stir in the pigeon peas mixture and the rice. Stir, add the stock and adjust the seasoning. Cover with a lid and bring to the boil. Lower the heat and cook until the rice is tender. Five minutes before the end of cooking time, add the olives and sultanas.

DESSERTS AND DRINKS

RICE WITH COCONUT

INGREDIENTS

2 COCONUTS

5 FL OZ (150ML) BOILING
WATER

MILK

1 STICK CINNAMON

4 CLOVES

4 OZ (125G) SHORT
GRAIN RICE

3 OZ (75G) MUSCOVADO
SUGAR

2 OZ (50G) BUTTER

THE COCONUT SEASON OR THE TIME OF THE *ECHADORES DE COCO* IS IN MARCH AND APRIL IN VENEZUELA. I USED TO SEE THESE COCONUT PLAYERS YEARS AGO IN SUBURBAN CORNERS OF CARACAS AND BUY FRESH COCONUTS WHICH WERE USED IN THE KITCHEN FOR PREPARING RICE AND OTHER DISHES. *ECHAR COCOS* WAS A GAME WHICH CONSISTED OF TWO YOUNG MEN STRIKING AT EACH OTHER'S COCONUT IN TURN TO SEE WHICH WOULD BREAK FIRST. IT IS NOT DISSIMILAR TO THE GAME OF CONKERS PLAYED BY SCHOOLCHILDREN IN ENGLAND. THE ONE WHOSE COCONUT WAS BROKEN FIRST WAS THE LOSER AND HAD TO GIVE HIS COCONUT TO THE WINNER WHO WOULD SELL IT VERY CHEAPLY. LENT AND EASTER WERE ALSO AT THIS TIME OF YEAR WHEN IT WAS CUSTOMARY IN CARACAS TO SERVE RICE WITH COCONUT AS A DESSERT. THE FRESH COCONUT MILK GIVES THE RICE A FULL FLAVOUR.

SERVES 2

Begin by cracking the coconuts and carefully, using a strong kitchen knife, separate the flesh from the shell. Grate the coconut flesh finely, using a food processor if available.

When the coconuts have been grated, add the boiling water and pass the mixture through a cheesecloth 1 or 2 tablespoons at a time, squeezing to get the last drop of the milky liquid. Make up to 1 pint (570ml) with milk if necessary.

Next add the cinnamon and cloves and bring to the boil. Add the rice and lower the heat to simmering point. Cook for 8–10 minutes, then add the sugar and stir to dissolve it.

Pour the mixture into a baking dish and bake in a pre-heated oven 350F/180C/Gas 4 for 45–50 minutes. Serve dotted with butter.

CHINESE NEW YEAR RICE

INGREDIENTS

This eight-treasure rice pudding is the traditional New Year dessert in China. With eight different fruits and nuts and bathed in syrup, this pudding is quite delicious.

16 FL OZ (450ML) WATER

8 FL OZ (225ML) SHORT GRAIN RICE

SALT

2 OZ (50G) BUTTER

1 OZ (25G) SUGAR

1 OZ (25G) SULTANAS

2 OZ (50G) DATES, STONED AND CHOPPED

2 OZ (50G) DRIED FIGS, CHOPPED

2 OZ (50G) DRIED APRICOTS, CHOPPED

2 OZ (50G) PRUNES, CHOPPED

1 OZ (25G) GLACE CHERRIES

1 OZ (25G) WALNUTS, ROUGHLY CHOPPED

8 OZ (225G) SWEET CHESTNUT PUREE

4 TABLESPOONS GOLDEN SYRUP MIXED WITH 1 TABLESPOON RICE WINE

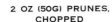

SERVES 6

Bring the water to the boil and add the rice with a pinch of salt. Cover with a lid, lower the heat and cook the rice very gently for 15 minutes. When the rice is tender, but not dry, add the sugar and stir once. Add 1½ oz (40g) of butter to the rice and set aside.

Use the rest of the butter to grease a steaming mould or pudding basin. Spread a layer of rice on the bottom and round the sides of the mould. Place the fruit and walnuts on top of the rice and try to cover the sides as well. Add another layer of rice and spread the chestnut purée on top. Finish with another layer of rice.

Cover the mould with foil or waxed paper and tie with a string. Steam the pudding for 1½ hours. Before serving, pour the syrup mixed with the wine over the pudding.

RICE MERINGUE

INGREDIENTS

6 OZ (175G) SHORT
GRAIN RICE

1½ PINTS (900ML) MILK

RIND OF HALF A LEMON

3 OZ (75G) CASTER
SUGAR

5 APPLES, PEELED,
CORED AND SLICED

3 FL OZ (75G) MARSALA
WINE

1 OZ (25G) BUTTER,
GRATED

1 OZ (25G) SULTANAS

½ TEASPOON VANILLA
ESSENCE

1 OZ (25G) PISTACHIOS,
COARSELY CHOPPED

3 EGG WHITES

1 TABLESPOON ICING
SUGAR

SERVES 4–5

First boil the rice in plenty of slightly salted water for about 5 minutes and then drain it. Bring the milk to boiling point and add the rice and lemon rind. Simmer for 5 minutes. Then add half the caster sugar and continue simmering until the rice is tender and creamy. Discard the lemon rind and let the rice rest.

While the rice is cooking, place the slices of apple in a saucepan with four tablespoons of water, the Marsala, butter and the rest of the caster sugar. Bring to the boil and then lower the heat. At this point add the sultanas and vanilla essence. Cook very gently until the apples are just tender and the liquid has been absorbed.

Spoon the rice into a lightly greased baking dish, spreading it evenly. Spread the apples and pistachios on top of the rice. Then whisk the egg whites to stiff peaks, adding the icing sugar during the whisking. Spread this meringue on top of the layer of apples and pistachios. Make some decorative swirls with a broad blade knife. Bake in a pre-heated oven 300F/150C/Gas 2 until the meringue is a pale golden colour.

THIS DELICIOUS ITALIAN DESSERT IS RICH AND A LITTLE GOES A LONG WAY. THERE IS A SIMILAR DISH IN PROVENCE, *POMMES AU RIZ MERINGUE*, BUT I PREFER THE ITALIAN ONE MADE WITH COX APPLES WITH THEIR FIRM, CRISP, AROMATIC FLESH IN HARMONY WITH THE SWEET, CREAMY RICE.

VENEZUELAN RICE WITH MILK

In Venezuela, Rice with Milk is as traditional as rice with coconut. You can prepare it at any time, whereas Rice with Coconut is regarded as a Lent and Easter dessert. Both puddings are mentioned in children's songs and games of long ago. There is a slight similarity between this rice with milk and the Arab *Roz bi halib*. I wonder if the Moors' way of cooking somehow managed to travel to Latin America with the Conquistadorès.

SERVES 4

Place the rice with the milk and the cinnamon stick in a saucepan and bring to simmering point. Cook very gently for about 10 minutes, then remove the cinnamon stick. Add the sugar and butter and stir for 2 minutes very gently. Add the raisins and cream.

Spoon the rice into a lightly buttered baking dish and place it in a pre-heated oven 300F/150C/Gas 2 for 30 minutes. Sprinkle with ground cinnamon just before serving.

INGREDIENTS

4 FL OZ (125ML) SHORT GRAIN RICE

1½ PINTS (900ML) MILK

1 STICK CINNAMON

2 OZ (50G) SUGAR

1 OZ (25G) BUTTER, PLUS EXTRA FOR GREASING

1 OZ (25G) RAISINS, SOAKED IN 2 TEASPOONS OF RUM

1 OZ (25G) DOUBLE CREAM

½ TEASPOON GROUND CINNAMON

RICE SOUFFLE

8 FL OZ (225ML) WHITE
RICE

2 PINTS (1.1 LITRES) MILK

SALT

1 OZ (25G) BUTTER

1 OZ (25G) FLOUR

3 LARGE EGGS
SEPARATED

3 FL OZ (75ML) RUM

3 OZ (75G) CASTER
SUGAR

THIS IS A LIGHT SOUFFLE TO BE SERVED STRAIGHT FROM THE OVEN WHEN IT IS GOLDEN AND PUFFED.

SERVES 4

Place the rice and 1½ pints (900ml) of the milk in a saucepan with a pinch of salt. Bring to simmering point and cook very gently until the rice is tender. Set aside.

In another saucepan, heat the butter, add the flour and stir for a few seconds. Remove from the heat and gradually add the rest of the milk, stirring all the time. Add the sugar, return the saucepan to the heat and cook the mixture, stirring until it becomes thick. Remove from the heat and add the egg yolks and the rum. Add the rice and mix well.

Whisk the whites of the eggs to soft peaks and fold carefully into the rice mixture. Spoon the mixture into a buttered baking dish and place it in a pre-heated oven 300F/150C/Gas 4 for 30 minutes. Serve hot.

RICE FRIED CAKES

RICE FRIED CAKES ARE PART OF MY CHILDHOOD MEMORIES. THEY WERE FREQUENTLY SERVED AT HOME AT LUNCH TIME. ALONG WITH FRITTERS, THEY ARE AN IMPORTANT PART OF VENEZUELAN COOKERY. BUT THE SAME CAKES, PREPARED IN ALMOST THE SAME WAY, CAN BE FOUND IN THE CARIBBEAN AND IN ITALY WHERE THEY ARE CALLED *CROCHETTA* OR *CROQUETTE,* SERVED WITH APRICOT SAUCE ON TOP, OR *FRITELLE DI RISO,* SERVED WITH SUGAR AS IN VENEZUELA AND IN THE CARIBBEAN ISLANDS. EITHER WAY, THEY ARE DELICIOUS WHEN SERVED HOT AND CRISPY.

SERVES 4

Place the rice and milk in a saucepan. Add ¼ teaspoon of salt and bring to simmering point. Cook the rice very gently for 10–12 minutes or until it is just tender, then set aside for 10 minutes. Mix the flour with the eggs and add the rice, sugar and lemon rind.

Heat enough oil for frying and drop in 1 tablespoon at a time of the rice mixture. Fry the rice cakes until golden. Place them on absorbent kitchen paper and keep warm. When all the cakes are fried, place them in a serving dish and sprinkle with icing sugar. Serve at once.

INGREDIENTS

4 FL OZ (125ML) WHITE RICE

8 FL OZ (225ML) MILK

SALT

1 TABLESPOON FLOUR

2 EGGS, BEATEN

2 OZ (50G) SUGAR

GRATED RIND OF HALF A LEMON

OIL FOR FRYING

ICING SUGAR

RICE WITH STRAWBERRIES AND CREAM

4 FL OZ (125ML) SHORT GRAIN RICE

1 PINT (570ML) MILK

SALT

2 EGG YOLKS

2½ OZ (65G) SUGAR

6 OZ (175G) DOUBLE CREAM, WHIPPED

3 OZ (75G) STRAWBERRIES

SERVES 4

Place the rice and milk in a saucepan with a pinch of salt. Bring it to simmering point and cook very gently until the rice is tender, then remove from the heat.

Add the sugar to the rice and stir until it is dissolved. Whisk the egg yolks, add them to the rice and stir again. Spoon the rice mixture into a buttered baking dish and place it in a pre-heated oven 300F/150C/Gas 2 for 25 minutes. Remove from the oven and let it cool.

Add the cream and half the strawberries, quartered. Spoon the mixture into small serving bowls and decorate with the rest of the strawberries.

THIS RICE DESSERT IS A LIGHT AND CREAMY DELICACY, SUITABLE FOR SUMMER DAYS. IT MAY BE SERVED WARM OR COLD.

ARAB RICE PUDDING

4 FL OZ (125ML) SHORT GRAIN RICE

1½ PINTS (900ML) MILK

3½ OZ (100G) SUGAR

2 OZ (50G) CHOPPED HAZELNUTS

SERVES 4–5

Place the rice and milk in a saucepan and bring to simmering point. Cook the rice very gently for about 45 minutes, stirring from time to time. Five minutes before the end of cooking time, add the sugar and orange blossom water. Stir and continue cooking until the rice is tender and creamy. Just before serving, sprinkle with the hazelnuts and almonds.

2 TABLESPOONS ORANGE BLOSSOM WATER

1 OZ (25G) TOASTED ALMONDS

CHICHA

This Venezuelan rice drink originates from the beginning of the century when many housewives and even nuns used to make confectionery and Chicha to be sold either at local grocery shops or by pedlars. The latter went through the streets crying out their merchandise: *Chicha fresca y helada* (fresh, cold Chicha). There is no more refreshing drink on a hot summer's day than a glass of Chicha with crushed ice. Nowadays the making of Chicha in Venezuela has been taken over by special factories, but you can still find a few Chicha-sellers with stalls in some central corners of Caracas.

INGREDIENTS

6 FL OZ (175ML) SHORT GRAIN RICE

2 PINTS (1.1 LITRES) WATER

10 FL OZ (275ML) MILK

4 FL OZ (125ML) SINGLE CREAM

½ TEASPOON VANILLA ESSENCE

SUGAR TO TASTE

SERVES 5–6

Boil the rice until it opens and most of the grains have disintegrated. By that time most of the water will have evaporated. Remove from the heat and allow to cool, then liquidise this pulpy rice in an electric mixer or food processor. Strain the liquidised rice through a cheese cloth, 2 or 3 tablespoons at a time. The end product must be thick and smooth, like custard.

Add the milk, cream, vanilla and sugar to taste. Stir to get it well mixed. Refrigerate for 1–2 hours before serving in tall glasses.

I N D E X

I N D E X